KEY CHAPTERS OF THE BIBLE

GOSPELS AND ACTS

Paul R. Schroeder

A Compilation
of Key Chapter Gospels and Acts Booklets
for Personal Study

Publishing House
St. Louis

KEY CHAPTERS OF THE BIBLE

An unforgettable Bible discovery method consisting of 20 New Testament chapters:

Matthew 6: Prayer	Romans 8: Salvation
Matthew 28: Go	1 Corinthians 13: Love
Luke 2: Christ's Birth	1 Corinthians 15: Resurrection
John 10: Shepherd	Galatians 5: Freedom
John 14: Heaven	Ephesians 6: Armor
John 15: Growth	Philippians 4: Joy
John 17: Intercession	Hebrews 11: Faith
Acts 2: Spirit	James 2: Works
Acts 9: Paul	1 Peter 3: Family
Romans 6: New Life	2 Peter 3: Judgment

Twenty Old Testament Key Chapters to be published at a later date.

Unless otherwise stated, Scripture quotations in this publication are from The Holy Bible: NEW INTERNATIONAL VERSION, © 1973, 1978, 1984 by the International Bible Society. Used by permission of Zondervan Bible Publishers.

Copyright © 1990 Concordia Publishing House
3558 S. Jefferson Avenue, St. Louis, MO 63118-3968
Manufactured in the United States of America

1 2 3 4 5 6 7 8 9 10   99 98 97 96 95 94 93 92 91 90

To my wife, Sylvia
and our two children, Douglas and Dana
God-given gifts to me.

They are all and more
than any husband and father could want.

CONTENTS

FOREWORD

For the 30-some years that I have known Paul Schroeder, I have always thought of him as a capable and bold, creative and innovative pastor. He had a healthy respect for the customs and traditions of the church; yet he was always free to discover and experiment with new ways of serving Christ and getting the Word out to people.

Paul Schroeder has a strong conviction about the place of Scripture in the lives of people, both its power to bring people to faith and to sustain and nurture faith. These are reflected in his teaching and preaching, always clear and concise, and, I might add, simple and direct.

Knowing this about Paul, I was not too surprised when I saw the first published Key Chapter booklets and their "weird" pictures illustrating a key book, chapter, and theme. That's what I expected from Pastor Paul. Of course, some of the pictures seemed far-fetched, but as Paul suggested, that was precisely why they were helpful. People would remember them, and thus remember God's Word.

Try this: list the things you remember from your last worship experience at church. How much do you remember of the sermon? How much do you remember of the children's message? Usually people remember more of the children's message. Why? Because of what we see in addition to what we hear.

The church has always used visual aids. In the Middle Ages, the builders of Europe's great cathedrals employed huge stained-glass windows to illustrate Bible stories so that worshipers could remember them and share their message and power. Our Lord himself spoke in parables—visual stories—and filled his teachings with life-related images like salt, light, vines and stones, seeds and weeds.

Twentieth-century people are more visually oriented than previous generations. Raised on picture books and television, people today are more visual than verbal, more digest oriented than detail concerned, more terse than verbose.

So it seems to me that the approach of the Key Chapters concept as compiled in this book is a resource for our time and will serve the Gospel well. Key Chapters will help adults, youth, and children do what Rev. Schroeder intends, get into the Bible, apply it to their lives, and share the Word with others.

I want to encourage the use of Key Chapters and their "weird" illustrations. Let these images help you remember the Gospel of Jesus Christ, apply it, and share it.

Dr. Ervin J. Kolb
Executive Director (retired)
Board for Evangelism Services
The Lutheran Church—Missouri Synod

PREFACE

God's Word contains the answers to all of life's problems and needs. As we apply God's Word to our daily lives, the Holy Spirit strengthens us, our faith grows, and our lives are transformed.

But for many the Bible is a mysterious and complex book, too huge to tackle.

By selecting important chapters of the Bible (20 from the Old Testament, 20 from the New Testament) and focusing on them, I hope to encourage people to get into God's Word.

To help accomplish this, I have prepared a visual memory aid for each key chapter. The aids are purposely *weird* in order to increase retention. Each aid has three elements:

1. The *book* of the Bible
2. The *chapter*
3. The *theme* of the chapter

By studying the memory aid several times and focusing on it, you will recall the image and consequently the book, chapter, and theme.

Remembering these key chapters will enrich your daily life. It will also help you to relate God's Word to others. As you write greeting cards or speak with people, you will be able to apply God's Word directly to their problems or needs.

Each Key Chapter is presented in the same format:

1. *Background* for the chapter
2. *Key verses* of the chapter
3. *Thoughts on* the theme of the chapter

Bible classes and small study groups will find the third section helpful for discussions. The *thoughts* will provide a variety of applications upon which to reflect.

God will not let his Word return void (Is. 55:11)!

He will bless you abundantly as you meditate on his Word (Ps. 119:48)!

He will enable you to be a blessing to others as you spread his Word (Gen. 12:2–3)!

soli Deo gloria
Paul R. Schroeder

ACKNOWLEDGEMENTS

I wish to thank the members of the church I've served for the past 24 years—Our Shepherd Lutheran Church of Greendale, WI. Serving as their pastor has been a great joy and privilege. Their support and encouragement of my writing is deeply appreciated.

Thanks to John and Carol Markworth. Carol used her artistic talent to originally "put on paper" my weird visualizations and concepts. Their commitment and support of Key Chapters was a constant source of encouragement.

Thanks to Russ Larson for his editorial assistance in developing the initial booklets and for his encouraging words. He provided expert advice and was a friendly enabler to keep Key Chapters going.

MATTHEW 6
PRAYER

Explanation of the Memory Aid

1. The BOOK of the Bible:
   The *mat*.

   = **MATTHEW**

2. The CHAPTER:
   The *number* of people.

   = **CHAPTER 6**

3. The THEME:
   The people looking up to heaven in *prayer*.

   = **PRAYER**

MATTHEW 6: BACKGROUND

Prayer is a great gift of God! Through prayer we are in direct communication with God. He has promised to hear and answer us. What an enormous privilege.

When calling on the phone, we usually hang up if there is no answer. Some people pray that way. If God doesn't answer immediately, they give up. How unfortunate. When believers pray they're ready to wait patiently on God's timing as well as his will. Efforts to make God "perform" according to our will and timing should not be part of our prayers.

Christ has made it possible for us to approach God in prayer. He enables us to do so through the forgiveness of sins accomplished on the cross. He knows our sin, but he chooses to pronounce us holy— his children. We sinner/saints thereby approach our holy God believing in his Son. So it is that all prayer must be in the name of Jesus. Only through him do we have access to the Father (John 14:13–14).

Any person hoping to be greatly used by God must of necessity engage in constant and fervent prayer.

But how are we to pray? Both the Old and New Testament are filled with the prayers of God's people. We can learn from them. Better yet, Jesus gives us an answer. The disciples had asked Jesus to teach them how to pray. The sample prayer he gave them is recorded in Matthew 6—the Lord's Prayer.

KEY VERSES OF MATTHEW 6

Verse 6

But when you pray, go into your room, close the door and pray to your Father, who is unseen. Then your Father, who sees what is done in secret, will reward you.

The opening verses of Matthew 6 warn us about doing spiritual things (giving, praying, and later in the chapter, fasting) for our own personal glory or reward. The warnings are necessary because of our self-centered, sinful nature. Motives are crucial! We are to be doing these actions so that God will receive the glory. Pray, give, and fast for God's glory.

Verse 9

> **This, then, is how you should pray:**
> ***"Our Father in heaven,***
> ***hallowed be your name,***

Our relationship with God is like a child's relationship with a loving father. We bear his name. We keep it holy by holy living, according to his Word.

Verse 10

> ***your kingdom come,***
> ***your will be done***
> ***on earth as it is in heaven.***

We ask
- that God's kingdom of grace (his church) will expand and grow;
- that God's kingdom of power will rule here on earth as perfectly as it rules in heaven;
- that the Lord will return soon.

"Your will be done," these are certainly the most difficult words in the prayer. We yield our preferences and priorities to the will of God. This requires humility. Difficult? Yes. Worth it? Absolutely. Our loving God knows the future. As a loving God, he will do only that which is for our eternal good. Indeed, "Your will be done."

Verse 11

Give us today our daily bread.

God graciously supplies our physical and spiritual needs. "Food" reminds us of necessities, not luxuries. Receive it all with thanksgiving.

Verse 12

Forgive us our debts,
as we also have forgiven our debtors.

This verse is often misunderstood. It does not mean that we *earn* our forgiveness from God by forgiving others. God's Word rejects such an interpretation. We cannot earn or deserve God's forgiveness through anything we do. As God in his mercy forgives, we will be moved to also forgive. (See Rom. 5:8–10; 8:5–8; Gal. 2:20–21.)

James makes this same connection of faith and good works in his epistle (See Key Chapter booklet *James 2: Works*). Faith shows itself by forgiving others. If we are unwilling to forgive others, how can we claim that the forgiveness of Christ is in us?

When we have difficulty forgiving others, or ourselves, it demonstrates the need to refocus on Christ's forgiveness of us. His forgiveness will flow through us to others. (See Mark 11:25–26.)

Matt. 6:14–15 helps clarify: If Christ's forgiveness is in us, it will show by our willingness to forgive others. By forgiving others, our faith is shown to be alive and well.

Faith is a relationship with God. Without faith, we are not right with God and not enabled to forgive others. With it, we are right with God and enabled to forgive as we have been forgiven.

Verse 13

And lead us not into temptation, but deliver us from the evil one."

God doesn't tempt (James 1:13); rather, we ask God to keep us safe from the temptation of Satan, which would lead us to doubt God and away from faith.

God does at times test us to strengthen our faith and draw us closer to him (Heb. 12:6).

A simple test to determine whether an event in your life is being used by God or Satan (since any event can be used by either) is to ask, "Which way am I moving in my spiritual life, toward God or away from him?"

Discipline from God (Prov. 3:12; Heb. 12:5–11; Rev. 3:19; 1 Cor. 11:32) aims to be corrective in nature and is always given in love. (See Rom. 5:3–5.)

Satan is not content to harm. He intends to destroy! As a lion, he does not merely wish to bite you—he intends to devour you (1 Peter 5:8).

The ultimate goal of Satan is our eternal separation from God. Human power and strength cannot resist him since he is a spirit (Eph. 6:12). We must have the armor of God to be victorious (See Key Chapters booklet *Ephesians 6: Armor*). It is this protection and victory that we pray for in Matt. 6:13.

Verses 21, 24

For where your treasure is, there your heart will be also.

No one can serve two masters. Either he will hate the one and love the other, or he will be devoted to the one and despise the other. You cannot serve both God and Money.

You have to make a commitment. God will not share his place in your heart. He wants your whole heart, soul, and mind.

Beware of money. In a materialistic society, money can easily become a false god.

Verse 33

But seek first his kingdom and his righteousness, and all these things will be given to you as well.

God wants first place in our lives. He will bless.

Verse 34

Therefore do not worry about tomorrow, for tomorrow will worry about itself. Each day has enough trouble of its own.

This verse summarizes the previous nine verses. The useless and silly nature of worry is revealed. It is pointed out that pagans have such concerns. As God's people, we are invited to trust Him to guide us and provide for us. (See Ps. 37:4–5; Rom. 10:11; Matt. 7:11.)

THOUGHTS ON PRAYER

Day 1

THE EYE ILLUSTRATES a point in Matt. 6:22–23. When healthy, it sees clearly and plainly. When sick, it sees unclearly and dimly, causing confusion. We must fix our eyes on Christ; then our healthy eyes will see life clearly.

*   *   *

PRAYERS OF FAITH and an obedient heart go together (1 John 3:21–24).

*   *   *

TO WORRY is to live as if you were a spiritual orphan.

*   *   *

MARTIN LUTHER felt fasting was a good outward preparation for Christian living—a form of self-discipline.

*   *   *

THE MORE POSSESSIONS A PERSON has the greater the danger of idolatry, because the need to protect and care for possessions can become a form of slavery.

*   *   *

HEAVENLY TREASURES are not subject to any type of decay, rust, or theft. The faithful will not lose their inheritance. (See 1 Peter 1:3–5.)

PRAYER IS PERSONAL COMMUNION with God. Prayer is worship.

*   *   *

AREN'T WE TO PRAY for our enemies (Matt. 5:44; Luke 6:28)? Aren't we to pray for their conversion? Of course! But what if they refuse conversion? What if their heart is hardened? What if they are leading others to hell with a different gospel? We pray God's judgment upon them to prevent them from leading others away from God (Gal. 1:8–9; 2 Tim. 4:14–15).

*   *   *

THE LORD'S PRAYER IS BRIEF. There is no repetition. The attention God gives your prayers is not determined by the weight of the words.

*   *   *

GOD'S ANSWER to your prayer may be yes, no, or later.

*   *   *

Day 2

THERE IS NO PRAYER to God without faith in Christ.

*   *   *

TO RESIST SATAN you must have the armor of God. (See Key Chapter booklet *Ephesians 6: Armor*.)

*   *   *

WORDS COME EASY. God looks at the heart.

* * *

WORRY IS A DISEASE that can produce many ills, not the least of which is fear. The burden and weight of worry is a form of mental and spiritual suicide (Matt. 6:25–34). But God calls you to "Cast all your anxieties on him because he cares for you" (1 Peter 5:7).

* * *

PRAY
- in the Spirit (Rom. 8:26);
- in faith (James 1:6–7; Mark 11:24);
- according to God's will (1 John 5:14; Matt. 26:39);
- in the name of Jesus (John 14:13; 16:23).

* * *

MATT. 6:24 calls for choosing between God and money. In this decision there is no compromise.

* * *

ONE GOAL OF PRAYER is to continue to seek the will of God (Col. 3:1–2).

* * *

A PRAYERFUL HEART pours out thanks to God (Col. 4:2). Effective prayer time involves a large portion devoted to praising God. (See also Luke 17:11–19; 1 Thess. 5:18.)

THE LORD'S PRAYER is found twice in Scripture: Luke 11 and Matthew 6.

*   *   *

IF GOD KNOWS OUR NEEDS ahead of time, why pray? If your wife knows you love her, why tell her? It's the same type of question. God's omniscience is not to be a deterrent. We pray, not because we have to, but because we wish to respond to his command and promise. We desire to speak to God as our friend. God not only knows our needs, he desires to fulfill them (Mark 11:24).

*   *   *

THE HOLY SPIRIT prays for us. By his power we cry, "Abba Father" (Rom. 8:15–17, 26–27). We may pray boldly as God's children.

*   *   *

Day 3

MATT. 7:7: **Knock and the door will be opened to you.** This does not happen for unbelievers since they have no spiritual ability to come to God (Rom. 5:8–10; Gal. 2:20–21). These words remind weak Christians who feel their prayers are not being answered to be persistent. If the door appears closed, be faithful, be patient, God will answer.

*   *   *

THE EVIDENCE OF FAITH will be seen in actions (fruit). (See also Matt. 7:16–20.) God looks for obedience (Matt. 7:21–23).

*   *   *

PRAYER SUBMITS TO THE WILL OF GOD. (See 1 John 5:14–15.)

*   *   *

THE SACREDNESS OF HIS NAME is of major importance to God. Not only does he refer to it in the Lord's Prayer, he also issued a command on the subject.

*   *   *

THERE IS A THIN LINE between persistence and patience. God wants us to wait upon him. That waiting is to be active rather than passive, trusting rather than hopeless despair.

*   *   *

GOD IS AVAILABLE at all times to his people. Our God never sleeps (Ps. 121:4).

*   *   *

HERE'S A HELPFUL REMINDER: ACTS of prayer.
A = Adoration (Ps. 34:1)
C = Confession (Ps. 51)
T = Thanksgiving (1 Thess. 5:17–18)
S = Supplication (Eph. 6:18)

CHRIST INTERCEDES FOR US before the throne of his Father (Rom. 8:34). We have a High Priest.

*   *   *

Day 4

SOME THINGS that hinder prayer include

- willful sin (Ps. 66:18; John 9:31);
- pride (Luke 18:11–14; Matt. 6:5–6);
- asking for selfish passions (James 4:3);
- lack of faith (Heb. 11:6; James 1:6–7);
- not treating your spouse properly (1 Peter 3:7).

*   *   *

HERE IS A LIST of the negative side of worry contained in Matthew 6:

- It not only is needless, it is useless. Worry can't change a thing (v. 27).
- It causes you to forget your worth in God's eyes (vv. 26, 28–30).
- Worldly people observe that you are no different from them (v. 32).
- Worry replaces trust in God. Anxiety can preoccupy your mind and prevent you from putting God first (v. 33).

*   *   *

A SAMPLE OF A PERSISTENT PRAYER that was blessed can be found in Matt. 15:21–28.

*   *   *

WAIT UPON THE LORD. God's timing is often not our timing.

*   *   *

LUTHER FELT THE LORD'S PRAYER was often martyred by thoughtless repetition.

*   *   *

1 THESS. 5:17: **Pray continually.**
Our relationship to God in prayer is never ending.

*   *   *

WE ARE REMINDED to pray for others, even our enemies. (See Matt. 5:44; Col. 1:3; 1 Thess. 5:25.)

*   *   *

WATCH AND PRAY—these two go together. (See Matt. 26:41; Mark 13:32.)

*   *   *

HUMILITY IS NEEDED for prayer (Luke 18:9–14). When the heart is full the soul is tender.

*   *   *

Day 5

GOD PROMISES TO ANSWER PRAYER. This prompts us to do the following:

- Believe (Mark 11:22–24; 1 Tim. 2:8; Matt. 21:22)

- Forgive others (Mark 11:25–26)
- Ask in Christ's name (John 14:13–14; John 16:23)
- Obey the Lord's commandments (1 John 3:22; James 5:16)
- Ask according to God's will (1 John 5:14; Matt. 8:2; Luke 11:13; Luke 22:42; Rom. 8:28)

*   *   *

PRAYER CONNECTED to the will of God fosters confidence. (See 1 John 5:14–20.)

*   *   *

WE SOMETIMES FEEL THAT GOD answered our prayer when the result agreed with our wishes, and conversely, feel that God didn't answer when the result was not what we wished. (See Ps. 42:9.)

*   *   *

GOD LOVES UNITY among his people. He promises to be present where two or three are gathered in his name (Matt. 18:20). This does not imply that sheer numbers will force him to respond. He also promises that even the fervent prayer of one righteous person has his total attention (James 5:16).

*   *   *

THE WILL OF GOD INCLUDES

- the proclamation of the message of salvation (1 Tim. 2:4);

- that we lead a godly life (1 Thess. 4:3);
- that we be patient in tribulation (Matt. 16:24; Acts 14:22; Heb. 12:6, 11);
- that we oppose Satan and his works (1 John 2:15–17; Rom. 16:20);
- that we be faithful to the end (Matt. 10:22; Rev. 2:10).

*   *   *

AMEN means "Yes, yes! It is true!"

MATTHEW 28
GO

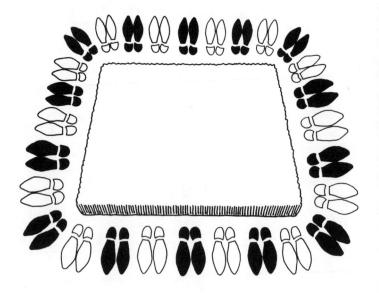

Explanation of the Memory Aid

1. The BOOK of the Bible:
   The *mat*.

   = **MATTHEW**

2. The CHAPTER:
   The *number* of pairs of feet.

   = **CHAPTER 28**

3. The THEME:
   Feet *pointing outward*.

   = **GO**

MATTHEW 28: BACKGROUND

God has given only one Great Commission to his church. He didn't give us six from which to choose. Just one! The Great Commission directs us to *go* to the entire world and make disciples for Christ. This is to be done by baptizing and teaching God's Word. The Holy Spirit will convert as we proclaim the message about Christ. (See "Acts 2: Spirit")

Other activities of the church (nurture, fellowship, service, worship, etc.) have their purpose and fulfillment as they relate to carrying out this one Great Commission—to reach the world for Christ through the Word! Nothing is of greater importance. Nothing is more urgent. Nothing else takes priority.

The church exists to bring us in, to build us up, and to *send us out*.

Are we willing to be sent? We have little difficulty speaking to others about things we know and love. As the Spirit of God grows in us through the study of his Word, our knowledge of him and our love for him will deepen. Our desire to witness will increase.

The world, without Christ, is lost. Jesus Christ is the world's only hope. God loves every person. He sent his Son to be our Savior. Now he wants everyone to be made aware of that fact. He wants all to know, so they can believe (Rom. 10:14–15).

That's why he says, *Go!*

KEY VERSES OF MATTHEW 28

Verse 6

He is not here; he has risen, just as he said. Come and see the place where he lay.

Other great religious leaders of the world have made powerful claims. They died. And they stayed dead. You can visit their tombs.

Christ died, but he didn't stay dead. He rose! He lives! He is true God!

Verses 7–8

Then go quickly and tell his disciples: 'He has risen from the dead and is going ahead of you into Galilee. There you will see him.' Now I have told you.

The women take the message to the disciples immediately.

Verse 10

Then Jesus said to them, "Do not be afraid. Go and tell my brothers to go to Galilee; there they will see me."

Jesus appears and directs the women to "Go . . . tell!"

Verse 15

So the soldiers took the money and did as they were instructed. And this story has been widely circulated among the Jews to this very day.

To this day, some people choose to disbelieve.

Verse 18

Then Jesus came to them and said, "All authority in heaven and on earth has been given to me.

Jesus has the highest authority. All things in heaven and earth must yield to him. (See also 1 Cor. 15:24.)

Verse 19

Therefore go and make disciples of all nations, baptizing them in the name of the Father and of the Son and of the Holy Spirit.

Disciples are followers. From every nation on earth there will come followers of Christ.

Verse 20

And teaching them to obey everything I have commanded you. And surely I am with you always, to the very end of the age."

The teaching of God's Word is necessary for our spiritual preservation and growth.

We do not "go" alone. Christ will be with us.

THOUGHTS ON GO

Day 1

MATT. 28:19 refers to the Holy Trinity—three persons in one true God.

*   *   *

SOME WERE CONFUSED and doubted—Matt. 28:17. They had not yet received the filling of the Holy Spirit. (See

"Acts 2: Spirit.") After Pentecost, they were bold and full of faith. They went to their death rather than deny Christ.

* * *

WE DO NOT PROCLAIM a dead hero but a risen Lord who *lives* (Acts 1:3).

* * *

THE EMPTY TOMB is the Father's stamp of approval upon the saving work of Christ (Rom. 1:4).

* * *

ANGELS WERE THE FIRST to announce the news of Christ's resurrection. The word *angel* ("messenger") is part of the word *evangelism*.

* * *

IF CHRIST HAD NOT RISEN from the dead, there would be no Christian church today.

* * *

JESUS COULD HAVE SIMPLY REQUIRED the disciples to believe in his resurrection without any proof. Instead, he chose to reveal himself to them after his resurrection. Not just once, but many times. Not speechless, but speaking. Not at a distance, but up close. The disciples, confused and skeptical at first, now were convinced. They had *seen* the risen Lord. He was *alive*!

THERE WERE 11 RECORDED APPEARANCES of Christ prior to his ascension:

1. Women returning from tomb (Matt. 28:9, 10)
2. Mary Magdalene (John 20:11–18)
3. Disciples on the way to Emmaus (Luke 24:13–32)
4. Peter (Luke 24:34)
5. Disciples except Thomas (Luke 24:36–43)
6. Disciples with Thomas (John 20:26–29)
7. Seven disciples by Sea of Galilee (John 21:1–23)
8. Eleven disciples in Galilee (Matt. 28:16–20)
9. More than 500 in Galilee (1 Cor. 15:6)
10. James (1 Cor. 15:7)
11. The apostles at the ascension (Luke 24:50–51)

St. Paul says he also saw Christ (1 Cor. 15:8). (See "Acts 9: Paul.")

*   *   *

Day 2

WITHOUT THE RESURRECTION, there would be no Great Commission. There would be no message.

*   *   *

THE COMMISSION is to mission.

*   *   *

JESUS KEEPS HIS WORD. He said he would rise; he did. He said he would come again; he will.

*   *   *

THE TWO MASSIVE PILLARS holding up the "arch" of the Gospel are Jesus' death and his resurrection.

*   *   *

THE GREAT COMMISSION given by Jesus is recorded (in different words) also in Acts 1:8; Luke 24:45–49; and John 20:21.

*   *   *

PRAYER IS AN ESSENTIAL PART of witnessing! Without Christ's presence and the Holy Spirit's power, the witness is merely words. (See "Matthew 6: Prayer.")

*   *   *

CHRIST'S RESURRECTION guarantees our resurrection. Our resurrected body will be glorified—free from sin and its effects.

*   *   *

YOU ARE TO GO! If not you, who? If not here, where? If not now, when?

*   *   *

TO BE A FAITHFUL WITNESS for Christ you need to know more than his teachings; you need to know him *personally*. You must know him before you can make him known (Phil. 3:8–11).

*   *   *

BAPTIZING AND TEACHING are the means by which the Holy Spirit produces converting faith. That is why we are to "baptize" and "tell."

*   *   *

MARY MAGDALENE and the other Mary had been at the crucifixion. They were the first to hear the news of the resurrection. Their response is an excellent example. They *believed*, then went quickly to *tell*.

*   *   *

THE JEWISH AUTHORITIES of that day tried every way to eliminate Jesus. They used trickery to arrest him. They used illegal means to try him. They used slander in their charges before Pilate. They always failed. After Jesus' resurrection, they used bribery (Matt. 28:12–15) to cover it up. They failed. Those who had seen the risen Lord were so convinced, so committed, that the truth was aggressively proclaimed. It hasn't stopped yet. It never will.

*   *   *

Day 3

THE COMMAND TO REACH the world would be impossible if it were not accompanied by Christ's promise to be with us as we *go* to the world.

God never makes a demand without giving the enabling power to obey.

*   *   *

THE WORD *all* dominates the closing verses of Matthew 28—*all* authority, *all* nations, *all* things, *al*ways.

* * *

"GO!" IS AN IMPERATIVE. We have no option.

* * *

SCRIPTURE repeatedly encourages, "Fear not." Those who trust in Christ need never fear.

* * *

FAITH IN JESUS COMES only as a gift from God. Physical evidence will not lead to faith unless accompanied by the Holy Spirit and the Gospel.

* * *

DISCIPLES ARE NOT BORN, but born again.

* * *

YOU CANNOT ACCEPT Immanuel's promise and ignore the process of going. The promise and the process go together. Christ promises to be with us. He assumes we will go (Matt. 28:20).

* * *

OUR TALENTS, BODIES, ENERGIES, GIFTS, AND POSSESSIONS are all to be used to carry out this one goal: to reach the world for Christ.

LET YOUR LIGHT so shine . . . (Matt. 5:16). (See 2 Cor. 4:6.)

* * *

OUR ENTIRE LIFE is to be a witness. Read the advice St. Peter gives to a woman who has become a Christian while her husband remains an unbeliever (1 Peter 3:1–6).

* * *

Day 4

JESUS REMAINS WITH US as our Good Shepherd (John 10), our Bread of life (John 6), and our Physician (Matthew 9). He constantly guides, supports, consoles, and forgives us. He surrounds us with his love and presents himself to us in Word and Sacrament.

* * *

IT'S FINE TO TALK about your friendly church, your pastor, or your choir, but you haven't begun to witness until you speak of *Jesus*!

* * *

WITNESSING IS NOT PRODUCED by coercion or force. God wants volunteers. The disciples were *invited* to follow.

* * *

THE MESSAGE, when "sown," will produce a variety of responses. (See Mark 4:3–8, 14–20.)

THE CALL TO DISCIPLESHIP is a call not merely to inner peace and joy but also to sacrifice and commitment (Luke 14:26–27). We are to count the cost (Luke 14:28–33).

* * *

WE ARE TO BEAR FRUIT (John 15:8). (See "John 15: Growth.") Witnessing is bearing fruit.

* * *

EACH TIME JESUS SPOKE of his coming suffering and death, he followed with a teaching on discipleship (Matt. 16:21, 24–27; 17:22–23; 18:1–4; 20:16–23). The connection is not accidental. Disciples must be ready to suffer for their faith. (See also 1 Peter 4:1 and Phil. 2:5–11.)

* * *

YOU ARE A WITNESS FOR CHRIST. Whether you wish to be or not. That's a fact. The only question is whether your witness is negative or positive.

* * *

YOU DON'T ARGUE people into the kingdom of God. You love them in by sharing the Gospel, which is the power unto salvation.

* * *

THE GREATEST "good work" (Eph. 2:10; Heb. 13:20–21) you can do is to glorify the Father by proclaiming his Son Jesus to the world. (See Key Chapter booklet *James 2: Works.*)

*   *   *

THE CHRISTIAN'S GOAL is to seek the lost. All of Luke 15 is devoted to that concept. The parables of the lost sheep, lost coin and the lost son teach us beautiful gospel. That's what the world needs. That's why we "Go!"

*   *   *

ALL LIVING THINGS MOVE. A living faith moves and goes.

*   *   *

ALL POWER BELONGS TO GOD (Matt. 28:18). *Nothing* can stop the spread of God's kingdom. It can be hindered. But, ultimately, God's kingdom continues to grow.

*   *   *

PREACHING AND TEACHING MINISTRIES must go hand in hand.

*   *   *

Day 5

WHAT ABOUT THOSE whose faith is weak and who are full of doubt? It's a terrible feeling! Maybe you've been struggling with doubt about God and his Word. Perhaps you hesitate to go to your Christian friends, fearing that you will upset them. You may wonder whether even your pastor would understand. You're a bit ashamed and mixed up about the whole thing. But one thing you know for sure—you have doubt!

First, let's make sure of what we're talking about. Some philosophers claim that doubt is a type of "belief" seeking more information. For them "doubt" means to be perplexed, to be puzzled, to be uninformed, to need more information, which would then lead to belief. For example, a young man says, "I doubt that what you say is in the Bible." He can resolve that type of doubt by searching the Bible on the subject under discussion.

Suppose you doubt something Scripture teaches. You don't need more information; it's simply that you have difficulty accepting what Scripture says. This kind of doubt makes you feel ashamed. You even wonder whether you are still a Christian.

The faith of our Lord's disciples, we know from the New Testament, was often at a low tide. On more than one occasion Christ had to remind his followers that their weak faith kept them from understanding and achieving.

Remember when the disciples came hurrying back to Jesus because they had failed to perform miracles of healing? The wind was really out of their sails. They wondered what had gone wrong (Matt. 17:14–20; Mark 9:14–29).

Christians of all times have their moments of doubt. Martin Luther said it was a usual and common thing for someone to doubt. He wrote many words about his own struggles with doubt.

Can a person be a Christian and still doubt? Yes! Many Christians have doubts in their moments of weakness.

You do not discover whether a person is a Christian by asking whether he doubts. You must know something far more important: what is his attitude toward his doubts?

The non-Christian nourishes his doubts and thrives on them. He boasts about his unbelief and takes great pride in his ability to question the Word of God. The believer, on the other hand, admits his doubt. He is struggling with it. He goes to God in faith to have his doubt resolved. He prays earnestly for the gift of the Holy Spirit to change his doubt into a strong conviction of belief.

Remember how Jesus dealt with the doubts of Thomas (John 20:26–29). He was kind and gentle. He lovingly confronted Thomas with the evidence. The Lord didn't strike Thomas down for his doubt. Rather, in love Jesus restored his faith.

Doubts are serious business. Treat them seriously. Talk them over with understanding Christian friends. Pray, "Lord, I believe; help my unbelief" (Mark 9:24). And he will.

LUKE 2
CHRIST'S BIRTH

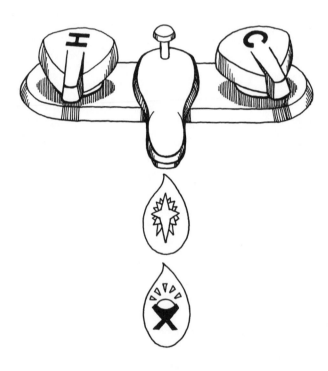

Explanation of the Memory Aid

1. The BOOK of the Bible:
   Hot and cold water makes *luke*warm.

   = **LUKE**

2. The CHAPTER:
   The *number* of drips.

   = **CHAPTER 2**

3. The THEME:
   Epiphany star and manger in the two drops helped mark the *birth* of *Christ*.

   = **CHRIST'S BIRTH**

LUKE 2: BACKGROUND

Luke 2 and Matthew 1–2 tell us of Christ's birth. Read both for the complete story.

Why was Christ's birth necessary? Well, let's go back to the beginning, Genesis 1–3. God, creator of all things, had created people perfect. There was a wonderful relationship between the Creator and his creation. Harmony prevailed between God and his people.

Then sin entered the picture. People were not content to be just people—they wanted to be like God. They yielded to Satan's temptation—rebellion and alienation resulted. People and God were separated. The harmony was destroyed.

Fortunately, God is a God of love. He still loved his creation and decided to give people another chance. He would give them an opportunity to be restored to the original harmony and perfection. God knew that Adam and Eve and all the people that were to become their sons and daughters could never accomplish this themselves—sin had destroyed that possibility. So it was up to God. *He* would have to save his people. There was no other way. God would have to send a Savior.

Since no human could fulfill the task of perfect obedience (which God required), God would send his own Son to do for all people what they could not do for themselves.

Christ would come to earth and take on human form. He would be God and man at the same time—perfect God and perfect man.

A sacrifice was necessary to pay the debt of sin. God is righteous and holy—the debt of sin had to be paid. The penalty for sin is death. So Christ must not only obey, he must also die. Obviously, Christ did not have to die for himself, he had no sin. So the Father counted Christ's death to the credit of those who by faith accepted his death in their place. He would die for them. Through his death they would be set free from their sin. God would cover their sins with the blood of his sinless Son and pronounce them forgiven and, therefore, holy.

God had this plan from the beginning. He didn't want his people to be lost. He gave them a free will so they could love. Freedom of choice is necessary in order to love. But people chose sin instead. God had a plan to redeem and save them. He told the first people about the Savior he was going to send. Those who believed in the Savior were saved.

Just as now, faith and trust in God were required then. It took faith for people to believe Christ was going to come. And it takes faith today to believe he has come. Both then and now faith in Jesus saves.

God's plan to save his people was put into action at a specific point in history. It culminated in sending his Son to earth to take on human form—the Incarnation.

Christ, true God, second person in the Godhead, always was—without beginning or end. He is true God—eternal. But now he was also "taking on" human nature. He had to be true man so that he could suffer and die. So Jesus, true God, true man, came to be our Savior. He came to do for us what we could not do for ourselves, take our sins away.

Throughout the history of the world, God sent prophets to keep telling the promise, "A Savior will be sent." The Christmas story is the record of God's keeping his promise.

He did send his Son, in the flesh, born of a virgin, Mary, to live, suffer, die, and rise again as our Savior.

The birth of Christ is directly related to Easter morning. Christ's resurrection from the dead shows the victory over death and Satan. He won! He did it in our place! Through him *we* have won.

God said he would come. He did. God said he will come again. He will.

Christ's first coming was humble and lowly—in a feeding trough. His final coming with his human nature will be in full glory and majesty—Resurrection Day.

Come quickly, Lord!

KEY VERSES OF LUKE 2

Verse 4

So Joseph also went up from the town of Nazareth in Galilee to Judea, to Bethlehem the town of David, because he belonged to the house and line of David.

God uses seemingly common daily events of history to work out his divine will.

Verse 7

And she gave birth to her firstborn, a son. She wrapped him in cloths and placed him in a manger, because there was no room for them in the inn.

Jesus was placed in a lowly, humble bed, a feed trough.

Verse 8

And there were shepherds living out in the fields nearby, keeping watch over their flocks at night.

In first-century Palestine, shepherds often found themselves at the low end of the economic ladder. Yet they, rather than prominent religious or government leaders, were the first to hear the angelic announcement. God often chooses to work with ordinary people.

Verse 9

An angel of the Lord appeared to them, and the glory of the Lord shone around them, and they were terrified.

Angels appear throughout Scripture to signal the unfolding of God's plan of salvation. Angels of God met Jacob. An angel appeared to Zechariah, an angel appeared to Mary, an angel appeared to Joseph several times, etc. Angels were present at Jesus' ascension. Angels will be with him when he returns.

Verse 10

But the angel said to them, "Do not be afraid. I bring you good news of great joy that will be for all the people."

God's gift, this most holy Gospel, this Good News, is for *all* people.

Verses 13–14

Suddenly a great company of the heavenly host appeared with the angel, praising God and say-

ing, "Glory to God in the highest, and on earth peace to men on whom his favor rests."

One of the privileges of the heavenly angels—and one which will be ours one day—is to be able to praise God before his throne.

Verse 20

The shepherds returned, glorifying and praising God for all the things they had heard and seen, which were just as they had been told.

Seeing Christ changes lives.

Verse 21

On the eighth day, when it was time to circumcise him, he was named Jesus, the name the angel had given him before he had been conceived.

Some people choose to use the name of Jesus in profanity, but a day is coming (the climax of the Lord's Day) when every knee will bow before Him.

Verses 27–32

Moved by the Spirit, he went into the temple courts. When the parents brought in the child Jesus to do for him what the custom of the Law required, Simeon took him in his arms, and praised God, saying:

"Sovereign Lord, as you have promised,
you now dismiss your servant in peace.
For my eyes have seen your salvation,
which you have prepared in the sight of all people,
a light for revelation to the Gentiles,
and for glory to your people Israel."

Simeon's hymn of praise has become a favorite of many Christians. The theme: God's gift, Jesus, is for everyone.

Verses 36–38

There was also a prophetess, Anna, the daughter of Phanuel, of the tribe of Asher. She was very old; she had lived with her husband seven years after her marriage, and then was a widow until she was eighty-four. She never left the temple but worshiped night and day, fasting and praying. Coming up to them at that very moment, she gave thanks to God and spoke about the child to all who were looking forward to the redemption of Jerusalem.

Those who are committed and faithful, like Anna, are blessed.

Verse 46

After three days they found him in the temple courts, sitting among the teachers, listening to them and asking them questions.

Of course, Jesus would be in his Father's house.

THOUGHTS ON CHRIST'S BIRTH

Day 1

SCHOLARS HAVE SPENT a lot of time trying to determine what the Star of Bethlehem was (Matt. 2:2). Books have been written suggesting various possibilities.

Perhaps, they say, it was the conjunction of the planets Jupiter and Saturn. Others suggest it was an explosion in deep space, a nova or supernova. Perhaps it was a comet or a bright star like Sirius. God may have prepared a special comet just for this purpose. Origen, a Christian writer of the third century, held that view.

God could have used something already there or something new. Either way, God used the Star of Bethlehem to spotlight the birth of his Son.

*   *   *

THE VIRGIN BIRTH is an essential part of Christ's first coming. If Christ had been conceived by man and woman, he would be only human. He was conceived by the Holy Spirit in a woman and is God and man.

*   *   *

Day 2

THE EXACT DAY OF CHRIST'S BIRTH has no significance, but Christians have picked a date to remember and celebrate his birth: Dec. 25. This was the date of an old pagan celebration of the "Unconquerable Sun." Some early Christians purposely chose to celebrate Christ's birth on Dec. 25 in order to declare publicly that Christ conquers all. By the end of the fourth century, most Christians celebrated Christ's birth on this date.

*   *   *

Thoughts While Visiting Christ's Birthplace

THERE ARE TWO BETHLEHEMS in the holy land. One is seven miles northwest of Nazareth in the territory of Zebulun. The Bethlehem which claims the honor of being the birthplace of the Savior is the one located in Judea, originally called Ephrath. References to this Bethlehem of Ephrath can also be found in the account of Rachel's death (Gen. 35:19) and in Micah's prophecy (Micah 5:2).

To this town came Mary and Joseph, both descendants of King David, shortly before Mary was to give birth to the Christ Child. It had been a rough three days' journey, but it was necessary. The order had gone out that everyone was to return to their city of ancestry. (When the Roman emperor told you to do something, you did it.)

Already at the time of Moses the Hebrews had a type of taxation (Ex. 30:12–13; Num. 1:18). Now it was Herod the Great's turn, and he was going to collect the taxes due Rome. (Actually, Rome had two types of taxation. The first was levied on all types of goods and property, while the second type was a head [poll] tax which was levied against every male and also served to recruit men for the military.)

As you would expect, accommodations in Bethlehem were not adequate to house the great influx of people. Every place was booked. But a place had to be found. God was soon going to bring his own Son into the world, through Mary. At last a place was secured. It was nothing spectacular, but it was the last possible place—Joseph and Mary stayed in a stable. A manger was his bed. He who was the Bread of life was laid in a *feed trough*.

Here in Bethlehem God delivered his love letter to the world, using Mary's womb as his envelope. The letter said very clearly, "God loves you." God had gone way out of his way to prove the greatness of his love. Here was the evidence: God had sent his own Son to take on the form of man so that about 33 years later, through his suffering and death, humanity would be redeemed.

God had very carefully chosen the time to send his Son to earth—the time was right. Because of Alexander the Great, the Greek language had become the commonly accepted language of the then-known world. The message of God's arrival in Christ would find ears that understood the language. Rome was ruling the world during a prolonged period of stability. The Roman roads, built to help Caesar's soldiers move quickly to battle, would surely also aid the "soldiers of the cross" as they eagerly went to tell the message. God had chosen the time, and now he was acting. His Son was born on earth. Now to tell somebody . . .

When God announces something, he does a good job of it. The heavens opened and angels spilled out—messengers with great news. What a shock to the shepherds to see such a glorious sight! The angel told them God had come to live with man. They would find him in the town of Bethlehem, in a manger.

I wonder what our reaction would have been had we been one of the shepherds that night. Would we have analyzed the whole thing as being some sort of a mirage. Or would we have turned to our companions and said, "This sounds like pretty good news. Too bad we don't have someone to watch the flock so we can check to see if it's true. We certainly can't leave our sheep here alone. After all, this is how we make our living. Perhaps tomorrow morning one of us can go see if there's any truth to this whole thing."

God makes no mistakes. These shepherds listened and reacted immediately to the message. Quickly they dropped everything and set out for the little town. God had spoken—they had listened. No wonder God had selected them to be the first to hear the wonderful news!

God has many ways of announcing things. He chose an angel to announce the good news to the shepherds. There were some wise men in the East that he also wanted to inform, and this time he used a star. Matthew records the account in his second chapter. These men followed the star, first to Jerusalem and then to the town where Jesus Christ was born.

God is still announcing the good news. The message is proclaimed from every Christian pulpit each Sunday. Just as the news warmed the hearts of the shepherds and brought adoration and praise from the Wise Men, the Gospel today continues to overwhelm the Christian with God's love. God loves you and me and sent his Son to save us! Thank you, God!

*   *   *

Thoughts While Visiting Bethlehem

THIS LITTLE VILLAGE is much the same today as it was in the day of our Lord. Everything seemed calm, and people wandered slowly through the streets, going about their daily chores. Even the clothing of the Arabs resembled that which was worn by the people living in Bethlehem 2,000 years ago.

The Church of the Nativity was built on the spot traditionally thought to be where Jesus Christ was born. Built in A.D. 325 by order of Queen Helena, the mother of the Christian emperor Constantine, it is one of the oldest churches in the world. Many scholars agree that the tradition behind selecting this site is quite accurate.

Emperor Hadrian, in A.D. 135, tried to profane the then assumed site of the nativity of Christ by planting there a grove of trees to honor Adonis. There can be little doubt that this grove of trees contributed to the fact that the Christians in 325 felt that this was the exact place where Christ was born. The church was built over a small grotto (cave) in which a manger was located.

The "cave" location does not contradict Scripture. The Bible does not say whether the inn's stable was a room constructed from building material or a natural shelter such as a cave, underground or above ground. In those days it was customary to shelter animals in small caves along the sides of hills or mountains. The possibility exists that the manger referred to in the Gospel accounts of the birth of Christ was in a cave.

Yet this is sure, Jesus was born in Bethlehem, and laid in a manger because there wasn't room in the inn. In addition, we have the very old (and probably reliable) church tradition regarding the spot of his birthplace.

*　　*　　*

Day 5
Thoughts on Visiting the Church of the Nativity

AS I WALKED TOWARD THE CHURCH, my eyes fastened on the entrance. It is so very small. Only one person can enter at a time and only then by stooping way over. Some people mistakenly say that the doorway was made so small to prevent anyone from entering the birthplace of Christ without humbling himself. This sounds beautiful but is not factual. This particular doorway was built around 1500 to prevent horses and animals from entering and desecrating the church.

Upon straightening up, I found myself in the church proper, which is 100 feet long and 70 feet wide. The side walls are decorated with beautiful mosaics. At the far end is the high altar of the Greek Orthodox Church. On both sides of the altar, stairways lead down to the Grotto of the Nativity. Thoughts raced through my mind as I descended the stairway. Here I was probably near the very spot where God, who had taken on the form of a human, was born of the Virgin Mary.

Inside the small grotto (not much larger than the average living room) stands the Altar of the Nativity. The traditional spot of the Savior's birth is covered with a marble slab in which is embedded a silver star.

A Latin inscription on the star reads *Hic de Virgine Maria Jesus Christus natus est* ("Here, of the Virgin Mary, Jesus Christ was born.")

As people enter the cave, they kneel on the marble slab in which the star is embedded and silently say a prayer. After praying, most of the people bend down and kiss the star. The center of the star is hollow, enabling worshipers to place their hands through the star to touch the rock below.

I silently moved off to the side and spent much time reflecting on the Word of God that describes my Savior's birth, life, death, and resurrection. I felt extremely close to God. It was an overwhelming experience. Somewhere near here, I thought, God had been born so that he could die on the cross for us all, so we could live forever. Beginning here, in the person of his Son, God spoke to the world. God revealed himself as a loving God. He went so far to prove his love that he came to earth to demonstrate this message in person. God's desire to forgive us our sins caused him to do all this.

I knelt in prayer, thanking God for his great *gift*. I, too, as all visitors do, placed my hand through the hollow opening of the silver star and touched the native rock of the cave. As I silently ascended the stairway back to the main floor of the church, my heart was beating hallelujahs. God is a loving God. God came to save all people from their sins. God sent his Son to save you and me.

God's Word is true. He made a promise: He kept it. He promised to send the Savior: He did.

Of greatest importance to you personally are these facts: God loves you; he desires your salvation; Jesus alone gives you forgiveness and eternal life.

John 10
SHEPHERD

Explanation of the Memory Aid

1. The BOOK of the Bible:
   Think of a tractor: *John Deere*.

   = **JOHN** (the beloved)

2. The CHAPTER:
   The *number* of sheep.

   = **CHAPTER 10**

3. The THEME:
   Sheep need a *shepherd*.

   = **SHEPHERD**

JOHN 10: BACKGROUND

Throughout his entire gospel, John emphasizes the deity of Jesus.

Many images of Jesus are presented to illustrate the work he had come to do among us. The 10th chapter of John presents some of these.

Perhaps the best known of all the images of Jesus is that of the *shepherd*. It was a simple and popular way to illustrate the work of Jesus. In the early church everyone could identify with a shepherd since shepherds were part of everyday life. The application could be made easily.

Today we find it helpful to review what the work of the shepherd was, so we can see the spiritual application.

One of the favorite chapters of Scripture is Psalm 23. It is commonly called The Good Shepherd psalm of the Bible. Psalm 23 and John 10 go together. They present the identical theme. In contrast, Ezek. 34:1–10 presents the image of evil shepherds who do not care for nor protect their flocks.

Scripture shows us the positive characteristics of a shepherd and relates them to Jesus. By contrasting those positive characteristics with those of an evil shepherd, John highlights the beauty and greatness of Jesus the good shepherd. When those qualities are taken to their ultimate perfection, you no longer have a good shepherd—you have *the Good Shepherd*—Jesus Christ himself!

KEY VERSES OF JOHN 10

Verse 4

When he has brought all his own, he goes on ahead of them, and his sheep follow him because they know his voice.

A walled sheep pen was entirely enclosed, with only one gate. The sheep were kept from wandering off and wild animals were kept from entering in.

Verse 9

I am the gate; whoever enters through me will be saved. He will come in and go out, and find pasture.

There's only one *way* to salvation! Just as Jesus is the *gate*, he is also the *way*, the *truth*, and the *life* (John 14:6).

Verse 10

The thief comes only to steal and kill and destroy; I have come that they may have life, and have it to the full.

Jesus loves his sheep. His love for them produces *abundant* blessings.

Verse 11

I am the good shepherd. The good shepherd lays down his life for the sheep.

A hired shepherd will not risk his life for the flock, since he does not value them as being his own. Jesus values us as his own. He has laid down his life for us.

Verse 14

I am the good shepherd; I know my sheep and my sheep know me—Jesus knows those who are his, and they know him.

Verse 18

No one takes it from me, but I lay it down of my own accord. I have authority to lay it down and authority to take it up again. This command I received from my Father.

Jesus was not a sad victim of circumstance. He came to lay down his life for us willingly, knowing that only in that manner could we be saved.

Verse 27

My sheep listen to my voice; I know them, and they follow me.

Again the knowing is emphasized. He knows us. We know him by faith. We will follow him.

Verse 28

I give them eternal life, and they shall never perish; no one can snatch them out of my hand.

God's gift to those who are his: eternal life. No one can rob us of this treasure. It is secure in him.

Verse 29

My Father, who has given them to me, is greater than all; no one can snatch them out of my Father's hand.

The Father's hand (power) is greater than any enemy, making us completely secure in Christ.

Verse 30

I and the Father are one.

Clearly, again, Jesus refers to his deity. (See John 5:16–18; 8:48–59; 10:33; 14:6–14.)

Verse 38

But if I do it, even though you do not believe me, believe the miracles, that you may know and understand that the Father is in me, and I in the Father.

Again Jesus refers to his deity. He invites those who are having trouble believing their ears (words) to believe their eyes (miracles). This is the same invitation he makes to Philip in John 14:9–11.

THOUGHTS ON THE SHEPHERD

Day 1

WE HAVE AN ENEMY who uses every type of deceit and trickery to get us away from the Good Shepherd. Satan is indeed a thief (John 10:1).

* * *

IN THE OPENING VERSES of John 10, Jesus, in refering to himself, uses two different concepts:

1. Verses 1–5: Jesus refers to himself as the *true shepherd* who is the true owner of the flock. This illustration refers to a communal sheepfold—the type

65

that one would find outside a city gate, a sheepfold in which numerous flocks would be tended for a short time while the shepherd was on business in the city. False shepherds may try to make off with a flock that is not theirs. But the true owner of a flock would come in by the gate. As the owner called his sheep, they would separate themselves from the rest and follow their master. They know his voice and follow him lovingly.

2. Verses 7–10: Jesus now refers to himself as the *gate*. No one can enter his sheepfold without passing "through" him. As they pass "through" him he counts them and tends to any injuries or needs. The anointing of the head with oil in Ps. 23:5 can be understood in that manner. This pictures Jesus' own protection and care of his believers, his sheep.

*   *   *

PSALM 23:
The Lord is my shepherd, I shall not be in want.
He makes me lie down in green pastures,
he leads me beside quiet waters,
he restores my soul.
He guides me in paths of righteousness
for his name's sake.
Even though I walk
through the valley of the shadow of death,
I fear no evil,
for you are with me;
your rod and your staff,
they comfort me.
You prepare a table before me

in the presence of my enemies.
You anoint my head with oil;
   my cup overflows.
Surely goodness and love will follow me
   all the days of my life,
and I will dwell in the house of the Lord
   forever.

*　　*　　*

Day 2

NOTICE THE REFERENCE to sheep being "led" rather than "driven." Jesus calls us to *follow* him. Prior to conversion our will was in bondage to sin and Satan. In conversion, God works a change that sets us free. (See Key Chapter booklet *Galatians 5: Freedom.*) Led by the Spirit, the believer has freedom of choice.

*　　*　　*

BE CAUTIOUS of following strangers until you know which way they are going.

*　　*　　*

THERE IS ONLY ONE GATE into the heavenly fold: Jesus Christ.

*　　*　　*

OLD TESTAMENT PROPHETS spoke of the coming Shepherd (Is. 40:11; Ezek. 34:11–31).

*　　*　　*

WE ARE NOT BORROWED OR RENTED. We are *owned!* Thank you, God! (See Rom. 8:6; 14:8.)

* * *

CHRIST knows his sheep! We may have trouble at times distinguishing whose sheep are whose. Often they look so much alike. He has no problem—he knows the heart!

* * *

THE UNITY of the Father with the Son is stressed throughout John 10. (See "John 14: Heaven.")

* * *

JOHN 15:13: **Greater love has no one than this, that he lay down his life for his friends.** Christ laid down his life for us—something a hired hand would never do (John 10:11–13).

* * *

THOUSANDS OF SHEEP had been offered as sacrifices in Old Testament days. Now the Shepherd is sacrificed!

* * *

CHRIST'S LIFE was not taken from him. He laid it down (John 10:18). Note the answer Jesus gave to Pilate (John 19:11).

* * *

THERE ARE ONLY TWO reactions possible to Jesus—unbelief or belief. It was true then (John 10:19–21); it is true now! Chapter 10 closes, **And in that place many believed in Jesus.**

*   *   *

JESUS CLAIMED over and over again to be divine. Even his disbelievers and his enemies knew that was his claim. It was for that reason that they accused him of blasphemy. They knew he claimed to be God (John 5:18; 10:33).

*   *   *

WHEN PRIDE AND INTELLECT get in the way of faith, remember that sheep are not known for their brilliance.

*   *   *

NOTHING other than falling into unbelief can rob us of victory in Christ (John 10:29).

*   *   *

NOTE HOW JESUS USES SCRIPTURE to substantiate his claim. His reference in John 10:34–35 is from Ps. 82:6. The magistrates were called "gods" because the word of God came to them and equipped them for office, but Christ was the *incarnated Word* of God.

*   *   *

THE LIFE OF DAVID illustrates the shepherd as a defender of the flock (1 Sam. 17:34–35).

*   *   *

SHEEPFOLDS in Israel often incorporated watchtowers from which the shepherd watched carefully over the sheep (2 Chron. 26:10). The theme of watching and being on guard against the enemy runs throughout Scripture.

*   *   *

JESUS IS CALLED our Shepherd (Is. 40:11; Mark 14:27; 1 Peter 2:25; 5:4; Heb. 13:20).

*   *   *

Day 4

JOHN 10:16 emphasizes there is only *one* flock and only *one* shepherd. Outside the flock none are saved. The one flock, however, includes not only Jews but also Gentiles—all who receive him as the Messiah. Together, one flock!

*   *   *

JESUS SPEAKS of his resurrection in John 10:18. (See Key Chapter booklet *1 Corinthians 15: Resurrection* and chapter 2 in this volume, "Matthew 28: Go.")

*   *   *

To CLAIM CHRIST as your Savior and not "follow" him is to claim faith without producing works. Impossible! (See Key Chapter booklet *James 2: Works.*)

* * *

JOHN 10:25 refers to miracles Jesus did in the Father's name. Jesus healed the sick, cast out demons, fed the multitudes, cleansed lepers, and raised the dead.

* * *

IN ADDITION TO LEADING, the shepherd healed and provided for the flock. Ps. 23:2 refers to the shepherd finding good pasture and quiet water for the sheep.

* * *

THE WORD *pastor* is the Latin word for shepherd. Their example is Christ, the Good Shepherd, as they lead the flock (church) over whom they have been made overseers (Acts 20:28; John 21:15– 19; Eph. 4:11).

* * *

SOME EXPLAIN that the shepherd's rod and staff (Ps. 23:4) were beaten together to make a clunking sound during times of poor visibility. The sheep would follow even if they couldn't see, as long as they heard the sound. They had explicit trust and confidence in their shepherd.

We are called to follow even when we cannot "see"— perhaps especially when we do not see our Shepherd at work. That is the very essence of faith.

Day 5

THE CHURCH, indeed, has dangers from the outside; but of greater concern are false leaders within. Good Shepherd, protect us from both.

*   *   *

A PRIMARY FUNCTION of a shepherd is to care for the young. Christ expects us to treat new believers tenderly and with considerable patience. They are to be enriched and encouraged by the example of mature Christians.

*   *   *

1 PETER 5:1–4: **To the elders among you, I appeal as a fellow elder, a witness of Christ's sufferings and one who also will share in the glory to be revealed: Be shepherds of God's flock that is under your care, serving as overseers—not because you must, but because you are willing, as God wants you to be; not greedy for money, but eager to serve; not lording it over those entrusted to you, but being examples to the flock. And when the Chief Shepherd appears, you will receive the crown of glory that will never fade away.**

*   *   *

HEB. 13:20: **May the God of peace, who through the blood of the eternal covenant brought back from the dead our Lord Jesus, that great Shepherd of the sheep, equip you with everything good for doing his** will, and may he work in us what is pleasing to him, through Jesus Christ, to whom be glory for ever and ever, Amen.

*   *   *

Rev. 7:14, 17: These are they who have come out of the great tribulation; they have washed their robes and made them white in the blood of the Lamb. . . . For the Lamb at the center of the throne will be their shepherd; he will lead them to springs of living water. And God will wipe away every tear from their eyes.

JOHN 14
HEAVEN

Explanation of the Memory Aid

1. The BOOK of the Bible:
   Think of a tractor: *John Deere.*

   = **JOHN** (the beloved)

2. The CHAPTER:
   The *number* in the sky.

   = **CHAPTER 14**

3. The THEME:
   The stars indicate *heaven.*

   = **HEAVEN**

JOHN 14: BACKGROUND

John does not leave us in doubt regarding the purpose of his writing. He clearly states in John 20:31: "But these are written that you may believe that Jesus is the Christ, the Son of God, and that by believing you may have life in his name."

A major emphasis of the gospel of John is the *deity* of Christ. John records seven miracles Christ performed. He also records seven claims Christ made regarding himself as the great I AM: (1) "I am the bread of life" (6:35); (2) "I am the light of the world" (8:12); (3) "I am the gate" (10:9); (4) "I am the good shepherd" (10:11); (5) "I am the resurrection and the life" (11:25); (6) "I am the way and the truth and the life" (14:6); and (7) "I am the vine, you are the branches" (15:5).

Partly because of the soaring heights to which his gospel takes us, early church artists selected the eagle to represent John.

From the first chapter of the gospel, where John presents the eternal preexistence of Christ, till the end where he reports seeing the risen Lord (and in his Revelation account where he pictures the ascended Christ at the right hand of the Father), John urges his readers to *believe*. Their belief must be centered and rooted in the truth that *Jesus Christ is true God!*

John wrote his gospel approximately 50 years after the ascension of Christ. He reviews many pertinent facts and teachings regarding Christ. Among them are the Lord's promises to send the Holy Spirit and his promise to return—both addressed in the 14th chapter of John.

Jesus' return and the promise of heaven are the focal points of the future for all believers. The presence of the Holy Spirit comforts us (and sends us as he was sent) as we wait.

To see how the teachings of Jesus relate to each other, read the 13th through the 17th chapters of John as a unit. Observe how Jesus answers the many questions of his disciples.

KEY VERSES OF JOHN 14

Verses 1, 27

Do not let your hearts be troubled. Trust in God; trust also in me.

Peace I leave with you; my peace I give you. I do not give to you as the world gives. Do not let your hearts be troubled and do not be afraid.

In both these verses, Christ offers his personal comfort—indeed a peace "which transcends all understanding" (Phil. 4:7). I (like many Christians) often experience his calming presence in my most troubling times.

Verses 2–3

In my Father's house are many rooms; if it were not so, I would have told you. I am going there to prepare a place for you. And if I go and prepare a place for you, I will come back and take you to be with me that you also may be where I am.

Peter had asked Christ a question (John 13:36). Christ had not answered immediately. First he wanted to reveal to Peter an insight regarding his willingness to "lay down his life." Now he proceeds to answer the question of where He was going. Jesus explains that he was about to go back to the Father—but through the cross, conquering sin and death and all the barriers between God and people. Yet, he would not leave his followers destitute. He would return by the Spirit to give peace. Plus, he would make a final return on the last day.

Verse 6

Jesus answered, "I am the way and the truth and the life. No one comes to the Father except through me."

Beautiful! Now we see Jesus answering a question asked by Thomas. Jesus not only claims to be the way to the Father but also promises to lead his followers to the Father. (See John 6:44.)

Verse 9

Jesus answered, "Don't you know me, Philip, even after I have been among you such a long time? Anyone who has seen me has seen the Father. How can you say, 'Show us the Father'?"

Yet another question was asked, this time by Philip (v. 8). It is comforting to notice the disciples felt they could approach Jesus with such questions. His patience and love are also available to us as we struggle with unfathomable truths.

Verse 12

I tell you the truth, anyone who has faith in me will do what I have been doing. He will do even

greater things than these, because I am going to the Father.

The world will have a fuller exposure to Christ through the Spirit. Today millions are reached with the Word by the miracle of radio and television as well as by the personal testimonies of Christians.

Verse 14

You may ask me for anything in my name, and I will do it.

All genuine prayer is in the name of Christ and within the will of God. All true prayer is answered. (See "Matthew 6: Prayer.")

Verse 15

If you love me, you will obey what I command.

A simple statement of fact. (See the Key Chapter booklet *James 2: Works.*)

Verses 16–17, 26

And I will ask the Father, and he will give you another Counselor to be with you forever—the Spirit of truth. The world cannot accept him, because it neither sees him nor knows him. But you know him, for he lives with you and will be in you.

But the Counselor, the Holy Spirit, whom the Father will send in my name, will teach you all things and will remind you of everything I have said to you.

The Spirit of God is a gift sent in Christ's name. The Spirit not only comforts and helps us but also leads us into all truth.

I will not leave you as orphans; I will come to you.

Jesus will come again!

Before long the world will not see me anymore, but you will see me. Because I live, you also will live.

Because he lives, we will live also. Read John 5:24; Rom. 6:4; and 1 Cor. 15:20 to gain additional insight.

Whoever has my commands and obeys them, he is the one who loves me. He who loves me will be loved by my Father, and I too will love him and show myself to him.

Jesus replied, "If anyone loves me, he will obey my teaching. My Father will love him, and we will come to him and make our home with him."

Christ makes a promise (v. 21). Judas (not Iscariot) has a question (v. 22). Christ restates the point and expands the thought. Clearly Christ expects people's actions to prove the validity of their faith. (See Key Chapter booklet *James 2: Works*.)

Peace I leave with you; my peace I give you. I do not give it to you as the world gives. Do not let your hearts be troubled and do not be afraid.

Peace with God—what a great gift of God! He does not do his giving as the world gives—fickly and unreliably. His giving is certain, constant, and eternal. His mood does not change and his desire for us never falters. (See 1 Cor. 10:13; 2 Cor. 1:20; 1 Thess. 5:24; Titus 1:2; 1 Peter 4:19.)

THOUGHTS ON HEAVEN

Day 1

THE WORD HEAVEN is defined in various ways in God's Word (in addition to being a part of the created universe [Gen. 1:1; Ps. 8:3]):

- As the abode of God and the angels (Ps. 115:16; Matt. 6:9; 18:10b)
- As the place to which Christ ascended (Acts 1:11)
- As part of the new creation of a united heaven and earth after Christ's return (Rev. 21:1; Eph. 1:10)

The common denominator: heaven is being with the Lord—in the direct presence of God.

*   *   *

MATTHEW 13, in seven parables, describes the kingdom of heaven (kingdom of God). By means of these earthly stories we are taught spiritual truths. The following are the major parables:

† Parable of the weeds: Matt. 13:24–30, 36–43. The reference to the "Son of Man" in verse 37 does not deny the deity of Jesus. It was a prophetic title Jesus applied to himself. (See Dan. 7:13–14.)

Evil, when sown, may not be perceived as evil. Satan sows it, and it grows to do its destruction later. It will become known by its fruits. The plants may look similar for a while, but the fruit will be clearly discernible.

The gatherers were perplexed. Wasn't the church to be holy and pure? Where did the problem come from? It came from the enemy—Satan!

There is always a temptation to use force in stamping out error. History gives us ample illustrations of this: inquisition; heresy trials; witch hunts; crusades; etc.

Some patience is needed for a while. Both plants are left to grow side by side. But judgment will come. Until then there will always be some trouble and evil in the church. We must wait on the Lord.

No one wants a sloppy attitude toward error. Obviously error should be fought against vigorously, as Scripture teaches us. Just a reminder: ultimately it is the "Lord of the harvest" who will do the gathering. He will make no mistakes. He knows those who are his.

The ungodly are doomed (Matt. 3:10, 12; 7:19; John 15:6; Heb. 6:8; 10:26–27).

Believers are "children of light"—children of the Father of lights (James 1:17) in whom there is *no* darkness (1 John 1:5).

*   *   *

Day 2

† PARABLE of the hidden treasure: Matt. 13:44. Spiritual treasure is different from earthly treasure. In

fact, earthly treasure often hinders the finding of the spiritual.

Spiritual treasure is to be sought, although at times it may be found when the person is not looking for it, i.e., the Samaritan woman in John 4. At such a time the joy is even greater.

† Parable of the pearl: Matt. 13:45–46. There are various interpretations of this parable:

- Christ is the pearl—when we see him as Savior, we forsake all to follow him.
- The church is the treasure. Christ is the seeker. Christ gives his all for the church.
- The church is the treasure that humanity is seeking. People find the message of salvation and surrender.
- Christians discover a deeper spiritual insight (pearl), leading to a more complete sacrifice of their lives to God.

By far, I prefer the first interpretation. Nicodemus was such a seeker (John 3:1–21).

† Parable of the drag net: Matt. 13:47–50. Bad fish were those without scales or fins (Lev. 11:9–10) or those that were dead, putrid (Lev. 11:11).

There will be a judging and separating (1 Cor. 4:5; Matt. 18:17).

Final judgment will come from above (Matt. 13:41; 24:31; 25:31.).

The end for the wicked is God's wrath and judgment (Rom. 6:21; 2 Cor. 11:15; Phil. 3:19; Heb. 6:8; 1 Peter 4:17; Matt. 8:12; 24:51; 25:30).

*   *   *

FOR YEARS I have had the habit of looking toward the heavens as I pray. Some memorable nights in which I gazed into the heavens stand out in my mind. Among them was a night of prayer in the lonely Negev desert at the foot of Mt. Sinai. By contrast, on another night, Nov. 13, 1966, as I returned home from a lecture, I remember how the brilliance of the stars was dimmed as I passed small towns lit up with street lights and gaudy neon signs. How the world detracts us from seeing heavenly things as we should, I thought. You're not required to look heavenward as you pray, but it might help your focus. (See Ps. 123:1.)

* * *

Day 3

SCRIPTURE USES many figurative terms to describe heaven:

- Father's house (John 14:2)
- Sabbath (Heb. 4:9–11)
- Being with Christ (2 Tim. 2:11–12)
- Eternal inheritance (1 Peter 1:4)
- Eternal kingdom (2 Peter 1:11)
- Abraham's side (Luke 16:22)
- Heavenly Jerusalem (Gal. 4:26)
- Heavenly home (2 Cor. 5:1)

* * *

THE UNREPENTANT, unforgiven, are excluded from heaven. No sin will be present in heaven. Therefore, no consequence of sin—illness, fatigue, worry, fear, etc.

JOHN DESCRIBED his vision of heaven in Rev. 21:1–22:5.

*　　*　　*

JESUS TAUGHT three parables showing the urgency of being prepared for his return. They are pointed and direct, urging a sincere and genuine faith that reveals itself in actions. All three parables are found in Matthew 25: (1) ten virgins (verses 1–13); (2) talents (verses 14–30); and (3) sheep and goats (verses 31–46).

*　　*　　*

THERE IS NO OTHER WAY to heaven but Christ. There is no other way to be saved! Christ alone gives us access to the Father. To say there are other ways to be saved, to make Christ merely one of a number of "saviors," is blasphemy. He alone is God, and he will not share his glory with false gods. John 14:6 is a statement of fact, constantly reaffirmed throughout Scripture. (See Acts 4:12.)

*　　*　　*

JOHN 14:14 is not to be taken out of context. It is not a promise that God will do whatever the whims of a prayer might request. God does not invite dictation from us and will not be manipulated by us. The verse must be understood in its context. Note verses 15 and 21. These remind us that prayer must always be within the will of God. God is not a Santa Claus or a benign puppet. Instead, Christ comforts and reassures us we will always have those things we request *that are within his will*. In the same manner, he promises to never leave us, to send us the Spirit, and to take us to himself! These promises come from a loving God!

*   *   *

Day 4

CHURCH MEMBERSHIP and profession of faith are worth nothing if our lives do not reflect obedience. The obedience Jesus calls for in John 14:23–24 springs from his presence in our lives and the strength and comfort given by the Spirit whom God sends. (See "John 15: Growth.")

*   *   *

THE PRESENT UNIVERSE must be destroyed because of the presence of sin. These things will pass away and vanish to be replaced by a united new heaven and new earth (Eph. 1:10; 2 Peter 3:10–13; Rev. 21:1) which will fully express God's perfect will and holiness. Such beauty and majesty are beyond human imagination.

*   *   *

TWO PLACES only in which to spend eternity: heaven or hell. (See Luke 16:19–31; Rev. 20:15–21:1.)

*   *   *

ONE DAY (unless he comes before we die, which is quite possible), Jesus will call our bodies forth from the grave. No fear then! Just ecstatic joy!

*   *   *

ETERNAL LIFE is God's gift (John 10:27–28).

* * *

THOSE WHO INSIST on "earning" their way to heaven have rejected God's gift in Christ (Gal. 5:4–5).

* * *

JESUS GIVES a direct promise of eternal life to all those who believe in him (John 11:25–26). Do you believe this?

* * *

JOHN SPEAKS of eternal life already being the possession of the believer (John 3:36). It will be completely experienced after the resurrection.

* * *

Day 5

WITHOUT THE *WAY* you cannot *go*. Without the *truth* you cannot *know*. Without the *life* you cannot *grow*.

* * *

A PERSON CAN GET to heaven without money, fame, or friends—but not without Christ!

* * *

JOHN 14:6 MAKES it clear Jesus is the one-and-only way. Not one of many ways; not even the best of a few. He is the *only* way.

IT WILL BE GREAT to be in the multitude before his throne (Rev. 7:9–17).

*   *   *

WE DON'T HAVE TO FEAR the future. Jesus is already in heaven! He is even now preparing a place for us.

*   *   *

IT IS DIFFICULT for "lovers" to be apart. Soon we will be where Jesus is!

*   *   *

JESUS IS NOT A SECONDARY GOD; he is God!

*   *   *

IN THE REVELATION OF JOHN, chapter 21, we are given glimpses of the beauty of heaven.

*   *   *

TO JESUS THERE IS only one real test of love—obedience to him (enabled by Jesus making his home with us [John 14:23]). Obviously, much of what we glibly call love is not love at all. True love, obedient self-sacrificing love, is demonstrated by Jesus.

JOHN 15
GROWTH

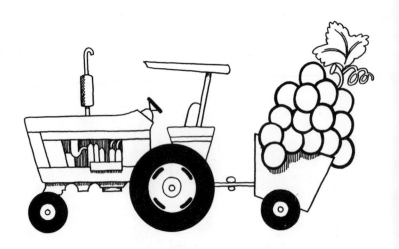

Explanation of the Memory Aid

1. The BOOK of the Bible:
   Think of a tractor: *John Deere*

   = **JOHN** (the beloved)

2. The CHAPTER:
   The *number* of grapes.

   = **CHAPTER 15**

3. The THEME:
   Grapes *grow* on branches, which depend on the vine.

   = **GROWTH**

JOHN 15: BACKGROUND

Growth, spiritual growth, is the theme of John 15. God wants his people to grow. God has designed all living things so that they grow. This is a universal truth: Everything alive must grow to stay alive. This is true of fish, birds, ants, elephants, flowers, weeds, carrots—all living things. There are no exceptions.

Humans also must grow in order to stay alive. If an infant stops growing, it will soon be dead. What about the elderly? Are they growing? Certainly! Their hair and fingernails may be all we see in terms of physical growth, but their minds continue to expand with new relationships and experiences. We equate a total lack of growth with death. We say of those who are not open to new experiences that they are "as good as dead."

The same is true *spiritually*. If we are not growing spiritually, we are dead spiritually. To be alive spiritually means to be growing in our relationship with God, in our faith, hope, and love.

Satan is a deceiver. Many who are spiritually dead are deceived into thinking they are still live Christians. Terrible! As long as they feel they already know *about* Christ, they will see no need to repent and become alive followers of Christ.

God has freely given us salvation through his Son, Jesus Christ. We cannot by our works or actions do anything at all in any way to merit this gift. It is free. It is undeserved. God's mercy alone has given us salvation. But once God has saved us and made us his people, he expects a response. He expects his gift to be taken seriously. He wants faithful people who really love him and want to serve him. He wants them to grow. He enables them through his Word and Sacrament so that they can grow.

In Biblical language the evidence of our faith is called "fruit." When alive in him, we grow and produce fruit. God doesn't want mere words of praise. He wants commitment, loyalty, obedience, and growth towards spiritual maturity (Eph. 4:13). The "end product" or "bottom line" of what we say we believe must be proved by what we do (James 2:17).

Matt. 7:21: **Not everyone who says to me, "Lord, Lord," will enter the kingdom of heaven, but only he who does the will of my Father who is in heaven.**

KEY VERSES OF JOHN 15

Verse 2

He cuts off every branch in me that bears no fruit, while every branch that does bear fruit he prunes so that it will be even more fruitful.

No dead branches are allowed. Producing branches are pruned, so they will produce more abundantly.

Verse 4

Remain in me, and I will remain in you. No branch can bear fruit by itself; it must remain in

the vine. **Neither can you bear fruit unless you remain in me.**

There can be no spiritual life separate from Christ. Where there is no life, there is no fruit.

Verse 5

I am the vine; you are the branches. If a man remains in me and I in him, he will bear much fruit; apart from me you can do nothing.

Christ is the source. We draw our strength and "fruitfulness" from him. He expects and provides an abundant crop.

Verse 6

If anyone does not remain in me, he is like a branch that is thrown away and withers; such branches are picked up, thrown into the fire and burned.

The unattached cannot live spiritually; therefore, they die. They are of no value; so they are destroyed.

Verse 7

If you remain in me and my words remain in you, ask whatever you wish, and it will be given you.

Our relationship to Christ gives us the marvelous privilege and blessing of answered prayer.

Verse 11

I have told you this so that my joy may be in you and that your joy may be complete.

God wants his people to be happy. Joy in Christ does not depend on circumstances. (See Key Chapters booklet *Philippians 4: Joy.*)

My command is this: Love each other as I have loved you. Greater love has no one than this, that he lay down his life for his friends.

This is my command: Love each other.

Christ's love in us produces a love for each other. That's why loving one another gives evidence of our faith.

You did not choose me, but I chose you and appointed you to go and bear fruit—fruit that will last. Then the Father will give you whatever you ask in my name.

God does the choosing. He has a purpose and plan for our lives. Our good works are to bring glory to his name. To that end he puts the gift of prayer at our disposal.

He who hates me hates my Father as well.

You can't separate God. If you reject Christ, you have rejected the Father also. Father, Son, and Holy Spirit are one inseparable God.

When the Counselor comes, whom I will send to you from the Father, the Spirit of truth who goes out from the Father, he will testify about me.

Christ promised the Holy Spirit would be sent. (See John 14:16, 26.) The Holy Spirit would lead us into all truth. The essence of truth is Jesus Christ— John 14:6.

THOUGHTS ON GROWTH

Day 1

IT IS NOT SURPRISING that Jesus uses the plant kingdom to illustrate growth. In plants we see the principle of growth—the miracle of life.

*   *   *

PLANTS CANNOT CARE for themselves. Neither can we. There must be a caretaker. God our caretaker is described in many metaphors. The Father is the gardener (John 15:1). Christ is shepherd (John 10:11–16). The Holy Spirit is helper (John 14:16) and truth revealer (John 16:7–15).

*   *   *

DIFFERENT SEEDS GROW at different speeds. The Holy Spirit does not operate according to human timetables. God's timing is always perfect. Trust Him!

*   *   *

PRUNING IS NECESSARY for a healthy, productive vine. Yet, from the viewpoint of the grape, pruning is traumatic. The cutting appears to be negative. We know better. Our intelligence is greater than a grape's. We know that the purpose of pruning is positive and productive.

When God comes into our lives to prune, do we

a. complain and murmur with the "understanding" of a grape?

96

b. in faith, accept God's promise that he is pruning us so we develop patience and endurance (James 1:2–4)?

Prompted by faith (2 Thess. 1:11), we should praise him in the confidence that he will deliver us in his perfect timing (Ps. 50:15; 34:17) and work everything out for our good (Rom. 8:28).

*   *   *

THE BEST FRUIT is love.

*   *   *

JAMES 1:6–8: **But when he asks, he must believe and not doubt, because he who doubts is like a wave of the sea, blown and tossed by the wind. That man should not think he will receive anything from the Lord; he is a double-minded man, unstable in all he does.**

A tree that is transplanted every day will find it's almost impossible to grow. A person who vacillates will have the same problem with growth. Sink your roots down into the Word! Fix your heart on Christ! Stand firm!

*   *   *

FERTILIZER DOES for plants what God's testing does for faith.

*   *   *

Day 2

GROWTH REQUIRES change. If you're not open to change, you won't grow. Tough, but true.

*   *   *

GOD IS INTERESTED in *quantity*. That's for sure. Look again at John 15: verse 2, "more"; verse 5, "much"; and verse 8, "much." Just as certainly, he is also interested in quality. We must abide in him for it to be acceptable fruit (John 15:2, 4, 5, 7, and 10).

*   *   *

WE CAN ASSUME an apple tree is "happy" having apples, a grapevine is "pleased" to have grapes. So, also, God wants us to have joy in doing good works. In addition, God wants his people to be joyfully confident even in difficult times. He wants his joy to be in his people (John 15:11).

*   *   *

THE GREEK WORD for "pruning" in John 15:2–3 carries the thought of "purging" or "cleaning." The heart must be cleansed (repentance and faith in forgiveness) before action is regarded as a good work by God (Acts 15:9). He looks at the heart. The motive must be love for God and a desire to glorify his Name. We do this most directly when we proclaim Jesus as the Savior of the world. As we show love to people, God is glorified. The more fruit, the more God is glorified.

*   *   *

MATT. 13:20–21: **The one who received the seed that fell on rocky places is the man who hears the word and at once receives it with joy. But since he has no root, he lasts only a short time. When trouble or persecution comes because of the word, he quickly falls away.**

Speedy growth is not always good, for it may lack roots.

*   *   *

WE ARE OFTEN INEPT at recognizing true good works because we cannot see the motives of the heart. We even fail to see some good works. And sometimes we applaud works that really aren't good in God's eyes.

*   *   *

Day 3

WITH CAUTION, we can sometimes evaluate our growth by comparing ourselves to others. Scripture encourages imitating some Christian examples (Heb. 13:7). It's safer to evaluate our growth on the basis of our personal response to God-given challenges and opportunities.

*   *   *

IT'S TOUGH to grow in concrete. You will grow best in the soil God chooses to plant you in. Grow where God plants you!

*   *   *

WE CAN'T TAKE any credit for our fruit. God prepared the soil, planted the seed, provided the sunshine and water, did the cultivating, and produced it all. *Soli Deo gloria!*

*   *   *

LUKE 12:48: **From everyone who has been given much, much will be demanded; and from the one who has been entrusted with much, much more will be asked.**

Small amounts of fruit are acceptable to God from young (new) trees, but a well watered and tended tree is expected to produce much fruit.

*   *   *

GOOD WORKS are often spontaneous, but it's also helpful to think about and plan good works. Prayerful thoughts based on the Word applied to human need will generate feelings and these feelings help move us to plan and to implement the doing of good works (Eph. 2:10; Rom. 7:4).

*   *   *

WHEN PEOPLE SHOW no fruits of faith—they don't pray, don't worship, don't witness, don't confess their sins, etc.—then they are not Christians regardless of how persistently they claim they are.

*   *   *

Day 4

GAL. 6:1: **Brothers, if someone is caught in a sin, you who are spiritual should restore him gently.**

Never despise or ridicule the person who grows slowly or slips back into sin. God uses his own measuring stick. That person needs your support, love, and encouragement.

*   *   *

GROWTH IS not always pleasant. Growing pains can be very real.

*   *   *

THERE ARE ONLY TWO TYPES of branches: producing and nonproducing. Either you are in Christ or you're not. There are no other alternatives.

*   *   *

GROWTH IN SPIRITUAL MATURITY does not necessarily follow chronological maturity. As Jesus pointed out, often a child may have deep trust in God, while an adult can be an infant in faith.

*   *   *

STEWARDSHIP IS usually one of the slowest fruits to grow. I've seen Christians with large fruits of faith in their worship, moral life, family, etc., whose stewardship fruits resembled raisins.

*   *   *

A CERTAIN FIG TREE looked healthy, but it had a serious problem: it didn't produce any figs. Jesus cursed the tree and it withered (Matt. 21:18–22). God is patient and long-suffering (Luke 13:6–9), but the time of judgment does come.

*   *   *

MORE FRUITFULNESS IS the reward for faithfulness in bearing fruit.

*   *   *

PRUNING TAKES TIME. Don't be impatient with God.

*   *   *

APART FROM CHRIST there is no such thing as a "good work" in God's eyes.

*   *   *

ARTIFICIAL TREES cannot produce fruit.

*   *   *

WITHOUT CHRIST we can do nothing. With him we can do anything.

*   *   *

NOTICE THE REPEATED EMPHASIS on love in John 15 (verses 9, 12–13). God's love for us is reflected and passed on as we demonstrate our love for one another. That's bearing fruit.

Day 5

Ps. 92:12–14: **The righteous will flourish like a palm tree, they will grow like a cedar of Lebanon; planted in the house of the Lord, they will flourish in the courts of our God. They will still bear fruit in old age, they will stay fresh and green.**
Spiritual growth continues throughout our lives.

*   *   *

2 PETER 3:18: **But grow in the grace and knowledge of our Lord and Savior Jesus Christ. To him be glory both now and forever! Amen.**

*   *   *

TUMORS, CANCERS—unnatural growths on the body—are harmful. Cares, worries, and guilts that fasten themselves to our spirit are harmful and stunt our spiritual growth. If not cured, they can cause death—spiritual death, unbelief.

*   *   *

WE MEASURE GROWTH in trees by a different standard than we measure flowers. God's assessment of your growth will be uniquely personal.

*   *   *

2 THESS. 1:3: **We ought always to thank God for you, brothers, and rightly so, because your faith is growing more and more, and the love every one of you has for each other is increasing.**

2 COR. 3:5: **Not that we are competent in ourselves to claim anything for ourselves, but our competence comes from God.**

Those who pride themselves in their growth are actually regressing.

*   *   *

MATT. 13:31–32: **He told them another parable: "The kingdom of heaven is like a mustard seed, which a man took and planted in his field. Though it is the smallest of all your seeds, yet when it grows, it is the largest of garden plants and becomes a tree, so that the birds of the air come and perch in its branches."**

We can be certain that God's kingdom will expand and grow. God's Spirit will see to that. The same Spirit of God has also brought us to faith. He also desires our growth.

*   *   *

1 COR. 15:10: **But by the grace of God I am what I am, and his grace to me was not without effect. No, I worked harder than all of them—yet not I, but the grace of God that was with me.**

*   *   *

EPH. 4:16: **From him the whole body, joined and held together by every supporting ligament, grows and builds itself up in love, as each part does its work.**

While individual Christians grow personally in faith, hope, and love, a group of Christians grows as a body.

JOHN 17
INTERCESSION

Explanation of the Memory Aid

1. The BOOK of the Bible:
   Think of a tractor: *John Deere.*

   = **JOHN** (the beloved)

2. The CHAPTER:
   The *number* of people in the church.

   = **CHAPTER 17**

3. The THEME:
   Jesus' hand (nail print) "lifting up" the church to show his *intercession.*

   = **INTERCESSION**

JOHN 17: BACKGROUND

John was very close to Jesus and knew him well (John 21:20, 24). John was present when Jesus went to Gethsemane to pray (Mark 14:33). He was present when Peter's mother-in-law was healed (Mark 1:29–31). He was present at the raising of Jairus' daughter from the dead (Mark 5:35–37). He was present on the Mount of Transfiguration (Mark 9:2).

John's gospel was written last, near the end of the first century. Already false teachings concerning Christ's deity had arisen. John wrote to refute strongly such false teachings and to give a firsthand, true account. His goal was that readers would be led to believe in the deity of Jesus (John 20:31). In every chapter the deity (as well as the humanity) of Christ is affirmed. John quotes five witnesses who declare the divinity of Jesus: John the Baptist (1:34); Nathanael (1:49); Peter (6:69); Martha (11:27); Thomas (20:28); and he himself makes the same confession (20:31). Under divine inspiration, John records for us the many events, teachings, and miracles in the life of Christ.

John also recorded (in chapter 17) the beautiful prayer of Jesus for his church. This longest recorded prayer has been called The High Priestly Prayer of Jesus because he intercedes to his Father on behalf of his people.

KEY VERSES OF JOHN 17

Verse 2

For you granted him authority over all people that he might give eternal life to all those you have given him.

In Jesus Christ *is* life eternal. He gives it away as a gift.

Verse 3

Now this is eternal life: that they may know you, the only true God, and Jesus Christ, whom you have sent.

This is life eternal: Believing in Jesus Christ. Those who believe in Jesus have crossed over from death to life (John 5:24).

Verse 5

And now, Father, glorify me in your presence with the glory I had with you before the world began.

Jesus is one with the Father. They existed together, with the Spirit, before the world began—three divine persons, yet one God.

Verse 8

For I gave them the words you gave me and they accepted them. They knew with certainty that I came from you, and they believed that you sent me.

Again, the believer trusts that Christ has been sent from the Father.

Verse 9

I pray for them. I am not praying for the world, but for those you have given me, for they are yours.

Jesus prays for us! He intercedes before the throne of the Father. He is our High Priest, speaking in our behalf.

Verses 11, 14–15, 21–23

I will remain in the world no longer, but they are still in the world, and I am coming to you. Holy Father, protect them by the power of your name—the name you gave me—so that they may be one as we are one.

I have given them your word and the world has hated them, for they are not of the world any more than I am of the world. My prayer is not that you take them out of the world but that you protect them from the evil one.

[I pray] that all of them may be one, Father, just as you are in me and I am in you. May they also be in us so that the world may believe that you have sent me. I have given them the glory that you gave me, that they may be one as we are one: I in them and you in me. May they be brought to complete unity to let the world know that you sent me and have loved them even as you have loved me.

As Christ prepares to ascend (return) to the Father, he prays for our protection since we still will be in the world. Strengthened by God's Spirit, Christians will support and encourage each other. He intercedes for the unity of his flock. (See John 10:16.)

I am coming to you now, but I say these things while I am still in the world, so that they may have the full measure of my joy within them.

Christ desires joy for his people. The joy comes through what Jesus says, his Word. (See Key Chapter booklet *Philippians 4: Joy.*)

Verse 17

Sanctify them by the truth; your word is truth.

It's a simple fact: *God is truth.* God declares you holy and transforms your life by the Word.

Verse 18

As you sent me into the world, I have sent them into the world.

The Great Commission in its simplest form.

Verse 20

My prayer is not for them alone. I pray also for those who will believe in me through their message.

God's Spirit uses the proclaimed Word to convert people and bring about faith and obedience. (See Rom. 16:26.)

Verse 24

Father, I want those you have given me to be with me where I am, and to see my glory, the glory you have given me because you loved me before the creation of the world.

Jesus longs for us to be in heaven with Him. (See "John 14: Heaven.") The verse also refers to the eternalness (deity) of Jesus.

Verse 26

I have made you known to them, and will continue to make you known in order that the love you have for me may be in them and that I myself may be in them.

God's love for us is known through the Word. Through that Word Jesus gives himself to be present in our lives. (See Col. 3:16.) His presence in our lives through the indwelling Word produces love for God and for all.

THOUGHTS ON INTERCESSION

Day 1

JESUS KNEW we would have problems in this world. He acknowledges that in his final words before his prayer (John 16:33). But notice that even then he ends with a Gospel word of comfort and hope.

*   *   *

JOHN 15, which describes Jesus as the vine and believers as the branches, also focuses on the unity Christ desires for his people.

*   *   *

THE THREE PERSONS in the Trinity and their *unity* as *one* God is indeed a mystery beyond all human comprehension. Yet, all three are involved in bringing us to faith in the one God. We know Christ and the Father only through the Word and the gift of faith from the Spirit. God's gift of his Son, and the faith to believe in him, both come from God.

* * *

IN CHRIST, we (his church) are to be one in thought, purpose, will, and action (Phil. 2:5).

* * *

THE HOLY CHRISTIAN CHURCH is *one*—accomplished only through Jesus Christ, who makes us brothers and sisters through faith in him. The earthly form of the church has been sadly splintered and divided. I sometimes wonder, because of our sin, whether it will ever be possible to have a physically united church on earth. I think not. How unfortunate. The one church exists—it's just invisible to the eye. The one, true church of Jesus is all who believe in him. Christ prayed for Christian unity so that the world would believe that the Father had sent him (John 17:20–21).

* * *

CHRIST'S PRAYER was fulfilled by his own suffering, death, and resurrection. The church is one. We are his body. (See Eph. 4:3–6; 1 Cor. 12:12–13.) We demonstrate our oneness by showing love to one another (John 13:34–35).

* * *

AN OLD COUPLET poses a thoughtful question about our individual responsibility in presenting the "image" of the church to the world:

What sort of church would my church be

If every member were just like me?

SIX TIMES in his prayer Jesus refers to his being sent by his Father. We hear that theme throughout John's gospel. It is mentioned 40 more times. Salvation is God's gift to us.

*   *   *

JOHN 17:5 speaks of the eternal preexistence of Christ. (See John 1:1–2; Col. 1:15–18.)

*   *   *

IN HIS PRAYER, Jesus asks the Father to give to those who believe in him

- protection from evil (vv. 11, 15);
- unity (vv. 11, 21–23);
- joy (v. 13);
- sanctification—being set apart for God's work (vv. 17–19);
- reunion with Christ, to see his glory (v. 24).

*   *   *

JOHN 17:10 refers to the divinity of Jesus. He and the Father are one. Any believer could say, "All I have is yours"; but only God could say, "All you have is mine."

THE ONE DOOMED to destruction was Judas (see Acts 1:16–20). God foreknew that Judas in his freedom would betray Jesus and also hang himself.

*　　*　　*

THE BOOK OF ACTS tells us about the early history of the church formed at Pentecost. Notice both the fact and the manner in which the New Testament church emphasized and displayed its unity (Acts 1:14; 2:1, 46; 4:24, 32; 5:12).

*　　*　　*

WHEN A CONGREGATION is caught up in strife and division, not much good will be accomplished to God's glory. What James says in James 3:16 is true: **For where you have envy and selfish ambition, there you find disorder and every evil practice.**

*　　*　　*

Day 3

TO BE SANCTIFIED is to be made holy. When the Holy Spirit used the Word of God to produce our faith, he set us apart to do God's work and to give him glory. True, we are still in this world, but not of it (John 17:16).

*　　*　　*

UNBELIEVERS DO NOT KNOW God because they do not believe in Jesus. Believers know God because they trust in Jesus as God's Son, sent for their salvation. The ability to believe in Jesus is God's gift of faith. He has opened our eyes to see. (See Key Chapter booklet *Romans 8: Salvation*.)

*　　　*　　　*

TO BE SET APART from the world (sanctified) does not mean to isolate ourselves from people forever. That would make the Great Commission impossible.

Yet, we all have need to get away at times. Christ himself went off for periods of prayer and refreshment. I have visited many monasteries, both here in the United States and abroad. Some monasteries I have visited have been extremely remote, such as Mar Saba and St. George in Israel. I have also had the privilege of seeing St. Katherine's at the foot of Mount Sinai. I wrote sections of this booklet while on retreats at St. John's Abbey in Collegeville, MN.

While I enjoy the privacy, quiet, prayer discipline, and fellowship of believers at monasteries, I am unable to accept seclusion as a way of life. People cannot believe if they do not hear the Word, and they cannot hear if someone does not tell them (Rom. 10:14).

It is necessary to come down from the mountain and go back to the mission of reaching the world (Luke 9:28–36). We have the example of Jesus and his disciples. After their periods of seclusion and prayer, they returned to minister and witness to people.

As Billy Graham pointed out, mountains are for inspiration, but fruit is grown in the valley.

*　　　*　　　*

THOSE WHO ARE SANCTIFIED by Christ will be glorified with Christ. Sinners washed clean in his blood will share his glory eternally. (See "John 14: Heaven.")

CHRIST doesn't pray for our speedy death. There is work for us to accomplish in the spreading of the Gospel to the world. That's the primary reason for us to remain on earth (John 17:18).

*   *   *

CHRIST KNEW why he had been sent to earth (John 17:18).

*   *   *

THE VERY ESSENCE of heaven is to be with Jesus. His glory will fill the new heavens and earth (Rev. 21:23). The angels cannot behold his glory without covering their faces (Is. 6:2).

*   *   *

IGNORANCE OF GOD is the darkness that engulfs the world. Jesus is the light; he is the way to God (John 14:1–7; 17:3).

IT'S POSITIVELY AMAZING! The Father loves us as he loves his Son. That is grace beyond comprehension (John 17:23).

IN THIS PRAYER Christ prays for

- himself (vv. 1–5);
- his disciples (vv. 6–19);
- all believers (vv. 20–26).

*   *   *

JESUS WAS OBEDIENT to his Father even unto death. Jesus would return to the fullness of God's glory as he rose from the dead, ascended, and once again took his place at the right hand of the Father (John 17:4–5; 1 Peter 3:22). Our faith and obedience gives glory to God (2 John 6).

*   *   *

THIS PRAYER WAS the last occasion of Jesus' dialog with his disciples before he faced his suffering and death. There is no note of personal fear or despair. His concern was for his disciples.

*   *   *

Day 5

CHRIST IS OUR ADVOCATE. He intercedes for us (Rom. 8:33–34).

*   *   *

ROM. 12:1–2: **Therefore, I urge you, brothers, in view of God's mercy, to offer your bodies as living sacrifices, holy and pleasing to God—this is your spiritual act of worship. Do not conform any longer to** the pattern of this world, but be transformed by the renewing of your mind. Then you will be able to test and approve what God's will is—his good, pleasing and perfect will.

*   *   *

DISHARMONY IN THE CHURCH disfigures the body, the body of Christ.

*   *   *

1 PETER 2: 9–10: But you are a chosen people, a royal priesthood, a holy nation, a people belonging to God, that you may declare the praises of him who called you out of darkness into his wonderful light. Once you were not a people, but now you are the people of God; once you had not received mercy, but now you have received mercy.

*   *   *

HEB. 3:1: Therefore, holy brothers, who share in the heavenly calling, fix your thoughts on Jesus, the apostle and high priest whom we confess.

*   *   *

HEB. 10:19–23: Therefore, brothers, since we have confidence to enter the Most Holy Place by the blood of Jesus, by a new and living way opened for us through the curtain, that is, his body, and since we have a great priest over the house of God, let us draw near to God with a sincere heart in full assurance

119

of faith, having our hearts sprinkled to cleanse us from a guilty conscience and having our bodies washed with pure water. Let us hold unswervingly to the hope we profess, for he who promised is faithful.

*   *   *

1 TIM. 2:1: I urge, then, first of all, that requests, prayers, intercession and thanksgiving be made for everyone—for kings and all those in authority, that we may live peaceful and quiet lives in all godliness and holiness. This is good, and pleases God our Savior, who wants all men to be saved and to come to a knowledge of the truth. For there is one God and one mediator between God and men, the man Christ Jesus, who gave himself as a ransom for all men— the testimony given in its proper time.

ACTS 2
SPIRIT

Explanation of the Memory Aid

1. The BOOK of the Bible:
   The *axe*.

   = **ACTS**

2. The CHAPTER:
   The *number* of birthday candles.

   = **CHAPTER 2**

3. The THEME:
   The *Spirit*, often symbolized by a flame, gives birth to the Christian church.

   = **SPIRIT**

ACTS 2: BACKGROUND

After the crucifixion of Jesus, his disciples became frightened and hid. They could hardly become leaders of the early church with that attitude. Something had to happen to change them, to make a big change, to make a *life-changing* change.

At his ascension, Jesus promised to send the Holy Spirit to change them. So important would the Spirit's arrival be that Jesus instructed the disciples not to do anything until he came. They prayed and waited.

Acts 2 reports the fulfillment of this promise of Jesus—the Holy Spirit came. It was a glorious day in which God poured out his Spirit on many. It was dramatic and visible. Nobody could doubt that something of great significance was happening.

His arrival was life changing. The disciples, who had been fearful, now became bold and strong in their witness. The change was not a brief emotional high that would pass in a few days. The change was thorough, and they actually grew in their commitment to Christ as time progressed. Even at the time of their deaths, they strongly and boldly proclaimed Christ as the Savior of the world.

How exciting to review the birth of the New Testament church! God is the creator of his church. To this day we celebrate this at the Festival of Pentecost.

Pentecost has direct meaning for us today because God is the same. His Holy Spirit is the same. He still converts, still builds his church. To this day he is the one who instills faith and Christian living, and we look forward to his strengthening and sustaining work upon us and all believers in the future.

KEY VERSES OF ACTS 2

Verse 1

When the day of Pentecost came, they were all together in one place.

Pentecost was an Old Testament festival related to the Passover celebration. It was also called Festival of Weeks, and the Hebrew word *pentecost* carries the meaning 50 days. Specifically, it marks the beginning of the offering of the firstfruits. The events recorded in Acts 2 have now become the focus of the New Testament church.

Verses 4, 11

All of them were filled with the Holy Spirit and began to speak in other tongues, as the Spirit enabled them.

We hear them declaring the wonders of God in our own tongues!

This miraculous gift of speaking in tongues gave evidence to the gathered people that God was present. The miracle also enabled the disciples to proclaim the mighty works of God to those present who could not understand Aramaic.

Some, however, made fun of them and said, "They have had too much wine."

Some will always disbelieve.

In the last days, God says, I will pour out my Spirit on all people. Your sons and daughters will prophesy, your young men will see visions, your old men will dream dreams.

Peter was direct in his sermon. He pointed out that with this miracle God began fulfilling his promise given through the prophet Joel that the Spirit would arrive with the arrival of the Messiah's reign (Joel 2:28–32).

And everyone who calls on the name of the Lord will be saved.

Peter offered the Gospel of forgiveness. This forgiveness is offered today.

This man was handed over to you by God's set purpose and foreknowledge; and you, with the help of wicked men, put him to death by nailing him to the cross. But God raised him from the dead, freeing him from the agony of death, because it was impossible for death to keep its hold on him.

God planned from the beginning to save his people. Christ's death (v. 23) and resurrection (v. 24) are essential to the message of salvation.

But he [David] was a prophet and knew that God had promised him on oath that he would place

one of his descendants on his throne. Seeing what was ahead, he spoke of the resurrection of the Christ, that he was not abandoned to the grave, nor did his body see decay. God has raised this Jesus to life, and we are all witnesses of the fact.

Peter reminded his listeners that David believed a Savior would come. He held up Jesus as that Savior. Peter personally witnessed to the resurrection of Christ.

Verse 33

Exalted to the right hand of God, he has received from the Father the promised Holy Spirit and has poured out what you now see and hear.

Peter said that what they were seeing and hearing was the result of Jesus' sending the Holy Spirit.

Verse 36

Therefore let all Israel be assured of this: God has made this Jesus, whom you crucified, both Lord and Christ.

Jesus is the promised Messiah.

Verse 38

Peter replied, "Repent and be baptized, every one of you, in the name of Jesus Christ for the forgiveness of your sins. And you will receive the gift of the Holy Spirit.

Peter finished his Gospel message with an appeal for action. The Holy Spirit moved them to repent and be baptized. Peter announced that the Holy Spirit was a gift for them in their lives. God was available to all of them.

Verse 42

They devoted themselves to the apostles' teaching and to the fellowship, to the breaking of bread and to prayer.

The early Christians were faithful in worship, study, fellowship, communion, and prayer. In Acts 4:32–35 we are told again of the spiritual unity enjoyed by the early church.

THOUGHTS ON THE HOLY SPIRIT

Day 1

IT WAS THE HOLY SPIRIT that transformed the disciples from cowards into courageous witnesses. Even when their lives were threatened, they continued to speak for Christ (Acts 4:20).

*   *   *

EVEN PRIOR TO THE PENTECOST outpouring, the Spirit was at work. God chose Bezalel son of Uri and filled him, and others, with the Spirit of God, with skill, ability, and knowledge in all kinds of crafts (Ex. 31:3).

*   *   *

THE BIBLE SPEAKS of us *receiving* the gift of the Spirit. God does the giving.

FEAR CAN BE DEVASTATING. It can cripple and immobilize. The Holy Spirit helps us conquer fear.

Fear causes many people to build a shell around themselves. Their true feelings are therefore hidden. They become impersonal and uncommunicative. What a terrible price to pay, even though they need not fear another person's reaction to them.

This veneer is difficult to penetrate. Just as a baby chick can be harmed by a rough and careless breaking apart of the shell, so also personalities can be damaged by a careless forceful extraction of emotions from someone who is "closed" out of fear.

Nature has provided a safer way for the "chick" to break out of its shell. The warm, moist bottom of the mother hen creates the perfect condition for the chick to venture forth into a new environment. The inviting warmth causes it to consider exploring further. The softness invites. So, slowly, ever so slowly, it breaks free from its shell. It chooses to risk the newness because the environment is welcoming.

That's how God wants it to work with people too. Christ repeatedly urged his followers to "fear not." He wants us to be free. It is God's plan that we are to create in our families and in his family (the church) a climate of warmth and acceptance. We are to love one another. When we sense such love and understanding we will begin to risk letting down the walls that separate. We will risk letting our feelings become known. Openness will result. Communication will improve. Fear will be dissolved. Love will grow.

Through the forgiveness he offers in Christ, God has shown that he wants to have a warm, personal, loving relationship with us.

As we grow in his love we will be able to create the climate for others to break out of their shells.

*   *   *

Day 2

CONVERSION IS THE ACT of God the Holy Spirit bringing a person to faith. In John 3 this process is called "being born again."

There should be no question as to what the phrase "born again" means. It is accurately defined and explained in Scripture. It is amazing, therefore, that within Christendom there has developed some confusion as to the meaning of the phrase.

The confusion can be seen in the question "Are you a born-again Christian?" The Bible equates being born again with conversion. They are synonyms. If a person is born again, then that person is a Christian. If a person is a Christian, then that person is born again. The two are identical. You cannot be one without the other. This is what causes the confusion with the question "Are you a born-again Christian?" The question implies that you can be a Christian without being born again. The implication is that there is one brand of general "run of the mill" Christians and then another brand of Christians called "born again."

As we see "born again" defined in the third chapter of John, verses 3–6, and also in 1 Peter 1:3, we see that it is taught as a contrasting opposite of unbelief—very much in the same way that St. Paul uses the contrast between light and darkness. In texts that speak of being "born again" the contrast is between something born of the flesh, which is human and limited and dies, and something born of the Spirit, which is everlasting and which has its origin in God. The point is that flesh cannot produce something spiritual, and therefore if we are to have the kingdom of heaven, it must come as a result of God's giving us this second birth.

So the question "Are you a born-again Christian?" is redundant. Those in the charismatic movement frequently use the question. It is their way of seeking out those who have had a moving experience (such as the gift of tongues). They often claim that their previous Christianity was in question. But now that they have had this spiritual experience (equated with being born again) they feel certain of their salvation. When the phrase "born again" is used in this manner, it implies that there are levels of Christian faith or levels of belief.

While it is certainly true that there are levels of maturity and degrees of commitment among Christians, that should not be confused with the simple matter of belief or conversion. Everyone who believes in Jesus, regardless of how weak their faith or how childish their commitment (not to say childlike), has been born again. Any person claiming a relationship with Jesus Christ as his or her personal Savior is on the exact same "level" as any other person in God's kingdom when it comes to the matter of being dependent upon faith for salvation. Faith is always given to us by the mercy of God. It is the gift of God—not produced by our experience and not brought about by our decision. It is the work of the Holy Spirit.

Decisions, maturities, commitments, increases in good works, and discipline follow that second-birth experience and are a result of the "born again" condition.

* * *

Day 3

THE EARLY CHURCH grew vigorously (Acts 2:47). The believers' witness was spontaneous and urgent. Their actions also convinced the people of their sincerity. It was easy to see their love for one another. People had a reason to listen to their message. And, as they spoke of Jesus, the Holy Spirit converted.

* * *

GOD DOES IT ALL. He sends us a Savior. He moves us to repent. He gives us faith to believe in our Savior for forgiveness. He gives us salvation through the faith he has given.

* * *

GOD WANTS HIS CHURCH to grow. It is a universal design of God: All living things must grow to stay alive. This is true of fish, dogs, elephants, fleas, roses, weeds, birds, and babies. It is also true of our faith. For our faith to stay alive it must grow! That is the work of the Holy Spirit. He nourishes us on God's Word, which is the spiritual food to keep us alive spiritually. He also uses the sacraments (Baptism and Holy Communion) to renew us and strengthen us in our faith. As we grow in our commitment to God, our desire to share salvation with others increases. As we spread his Word, and the Spirit uses the message to convert, more and more people will be brought to faith. His church grows. Not even the gates of hell will prevail against it (Matt. 16:18). (See also Acts 1:8.)

*   *   *

ALSO FOR US, the Holy Spirit promises comfort and delivery—in his time and in his way.

*   *   *

JUST AS THE DISCIPLES received the gift of the Spirit on Pentecost, so every believer has received at least one gift given by the Holy Spirit (1 Cor. 12:11). The entire 12th chapter of 1 Corinthians speaks about these gifts of grace. These gifts are to be used for the welfare of the entire church. The analogy of body parts points to the purpose of the gifts.

*   *   *

Day 4

1 CORINTHIANS 14 addresses the subject of the gift of "tongues." Paul makes several things clear:

- "Tongues" are not the ultimate proof of one's faith. In fact, too much importance given to this "experience" can divert attention away from Christ.
- Those who have the gift of "tongues" are *not* "higher level" Christians.

- Speaking the Gospel in a known language is more important than the personal use of an unknown language.
- Caution must be used to avoid problems in the church (1 Cor. 14:22–28).
- Order and harmony are to be preserved (1 Cor. 14:33, 39–40).

* * *

PAUL SPOKE IN TONGUES, but he had his priorities in place (1 Cor. 14:5–12, 18–19).

* * *

THE HOLY SPIRIT is the Breath of God.

* * *

CHRIST JESUS' suffering, death, and resurrection fulfilled prophecy.

* * *

REPENTANCE COMES AS A RESULT of the work of the Holy Spirit. Both John the Baptist and Jesus called for repentance—a sign of conversion and faith.

* * *

THE BOOK OF ACTS also stresses prayer and its importance in the daily life of a Christian. (See Acts 1:14; 3:1; 6:4; 10:4, 31; 12:5; 16:13, 16.)

THE WITNESSING BEGUN in Jerusalem spread to Samaria and Judea (Acts 8–12) and finally to the ends of the then-known world (Acts 13–28). The Holy Spirit made the early church a going church—going with a message! (See also Luke 24:46–49 and Acts 1:8.)

* * *

Day 5

JESUS, IN THE GOSPEL OF JOHN, tells us about the work of the Holy Spirit: teaching (14:26); testifying about Christ (15:26); and convicting of sin, guiding in truth, and glorifying Christ (16:7–11).

* * *

THE HOLY SPIRIT is the comforter (Acts 9:31).

* * *

BELIEVERS, by rebellion and resistance to the Word, kill their own faith and thus can grieve the Holy Spirit. (See Eph. 4:30; Acts 5:3, 9; 7:51.)

* * *

PETER SPOKE PLAINLY and with guts. Though Peter spoke sharply, he spoke in love, calling them brothers (Acts 2:29). Pray for the freeing power of the Spirit upon pastors today.

* * *

REPRESENTATIVE GIFTS of the Holy Spirit are listed in three chapters of the Bible: Romans 12; 1 Corinthians

12; and Ephesians 4. Peter summarizes them and gives their purpose in 1 Peter 4:10–11.

* * *

It is the Holy Spirit who "marks" us as being the children of God (Eph. 1:13; 4:30; 2 Cor. 1:21–22.)

* * *

The Holy Spirit serves as our advocate in prayer (Rom. 8:26–27).

* * *

The sin against the Holy Spirit is a rejection of the Spirit's work of repentance and faith and is therefore unforgivable. (See Matt. 12:31–32; Heb. 6:4–6; 10:26–27; 1 John 5:16–17.)

* * *

Rev. 2:7: **He who has an ear, let him hear what the Spirit says to the churches.** (See also Rev. 2:7, 11, 17, 29; 3:6, 13, 26.)

* * *

Zech. 4:6: **Not by might, nor by power, but by my Spirit, says the Lord Almighty.**

ACTS 9
PAUL

Explanation of the Memory Aid

1. The BOOK of the Bible:
   The *axe*.

   = **ACTS**

2. The CHAPTER:
   The *number* formed by the cloud and lightning bolt.

   = **CHAPTER 9**

3. The THEME:
   As light flashed around him, *Saul* fell to the ground on the highway to Damascus.

   = **PAUL** (formerly Saul)

ACTS 9: BACKGROUND

His name was Saul. He was a proud Pharisee, destined to become one of the greatest men of all time. The story of his conversion is perhaps the best known in history. Born at Tarsus, Paul was probably in his early 30s when we first hear of him in the Scriptures. Luke mentions him as being the coat watcher at the stoning of Stephen (Acts 7:58). However, we get more of an insight into his fanatic zeal as we see him on the way to Damascus on a search-and-destroy mission against the new Christians.

God intervened. In a flash, literally, Saul's life was turned around. God changed his direction—which is what conversion is all about.

From that moment forward he became God's great missionary to the Gentiles. The zeal he used against God's people is now used to proclaim God's way of salvation through Christ.

Paul, as he became known, never forgot his conversion. He never ceased to be amazed at the mercy of God, who had come to save him while he was in the middle of rebellion.

Throughout his missionary journeys, Paul established numerous congregations. His vigorous preaching and teaching held up Jesus Christ the Savior for all to see. The great sermon in Athens illustrated his simple and direct style of preaching (Acts 17:22–31). Under inspiration from God, Paul wrote letters to churches and individuals throughout the ancient world. These letters constitute over one-third of the New Testament.

The life of Paul will forever be an example of what happens when God turns a person around and that person becomes turned on to God. He indeed was set apart for the Gospel of God (Rom. 1:1; Gal. 1:15).

As a theme for his life, Paul could very well have chosen what he wrote to the church in Rome recorded in Rom. 1:16–17, "I am not ashamed of the gospel, because it is the power of God for the salvation of everyone who believes: first for the Jew, then for the Gentile. For in the gospel a righteousness from God is revealed, a righteousness that is by faith from beginning to end, just as it is written: **'The righteous will live by faith.'** "

KEY VERSES OF ACTS 9

Verses 1–2

Meanwhile, Saul was still breathing out murderous threats against the Lord's disciples. He went to the high priest and asked him for letters to the synagogues in Damascus, so that if he found any there who belonged to the Way, whether men or women, he might take them as prisoners to Jerusalem.

Saul, as he was known at the time, was not seeking God. He was out to destroy the young Christian church.

As he neared Damascus on his journey, suddenly a light from heaven flashed around him. He fell to the ground and heard a voice say to him, "Saul, Saul, why do you persecute me?"

"Who are you, Lord?" Saul asked.

"I am Jesus, whom you are persecuting," he replied. "Now get up and go into the city, and you will be told what you must do."

Saul would never forget the significance of this meeting with Jesus.

Verse 12

In a vision he had seen a man named Ananias come and place his hands on him to restore his sight.

God let him know he would be healed.

Verse 15

But the Lord said to Ananias, "Go! This man is my chosen instrument to carry my name before the Gentiles and their kings and before the people of Israel."

God had singled Saul out for a special purpose— to bring the Good News of salvation in Christ to the Gentile world.

Verse 16

I will show him how much he must suffer for my name.

Those who serve the Lord must be prepared to suffer for his name's sake. (See Luke 9:23–24; 14:25–35.)

Verse 20

At once he began to preach in the synagogues that Jesus is the Son of God.

Saul begins the ministry that will extend throughout his life.

Verse 22

Yet Saul grew more and more powerful and baffled the Jews living in Damascus by proving that Jesus is the Christ.

The core of the message was *Jesus is the Christ.*

Verse 24

But Saul learned of their plan. Day and night they kept close watch on the city gates in order to kill him.

The foretold (v. 16) persecution begins.

Verse 31

Then the church throughout Judea, Galilee and Samaria enjoyed a time of peace. It was strengthened; and encouraged by the Holy Spirit, it grew in numbers, living in the fear of the Lord.

God provided a time of peace and growth for the church.

Verses 34, 41

"Aeneas," Peter said to him, "Jesus Christ heals you. Get up and take care of your mat." Immediately Aeneas got up.

He took her by the hand and helped her to her feet. Then he called the believers and the widows and presented her to them alive.

The last quarter of the chapter deals with the ministry of Peter; healing Aeneas and raising Dorcas.

THOUGHTS ON PAUL

Day 1

PAUL FREQUENTLY REFERRED to his conversion (Acts 22:4–19; 26:9–15; 1 Cor. 9:1; 15:8; Gal. 1:11–12; 1 Tim. 1:12–16). But his *experience* wasn't the heart of his message. Christ was his message.

*   *   *

"PAUL" WAS THE ROMAN NAME for "Saul." It's interesting that once Saul starts reaching the Gentiles, he is frequently called Paul. Luke refers to this in Acts 13:9. The Gentiles could more easily identify with the Gentile name Paul than the Hebrew name Saul.

*   *   *

THERE WERE UPS AND DOWNS in Paul's ministry. At times people listened and responded. At other times his life was threatened by their hostility.

*   *   *

PAUL WAS ANXIOUS to spread the message of Christ. He traveled throughout the Gentile world to proclaim Jesus. Among the places where he preached were Salamis (Acts 13:5), Paphos (Acts 13:6); Antioch in Pisidia (Acts 13:14–51), and Macedonia (Acts 16:6–10).

The new believers at Philippi, Thessalonica, Corinth, Ephesus, as well as Rome were nourished and instructed by him. God used Paul as the founder of these new congregations of believers. His personal love and concern can be seen in his later letters to them.

* * *

THE DISCIPLES WERE SUSPICIOUS concerning the authenticity of Paul's conversion (Acts 9:26). Barnabas helped Paul win the acceptance of the others (v. 27).

* * *

Day 2

PAUL SPENT THREE YEARS in the Arabian desert to be prepared for his ministry. This was a time alone with God (Gal. 1:17).

* * *

THE FIRST CONVERT to Christianity in Europe was a businesswoman named Lydia, a seller of fabric (Acts 16:14).

* * *

PAUL WAS A MAN of great courage. In Athens (while preaching at the Areopagus in full view of the Parthenon, which contained the gold and ivory statue of Athene), he denounced the temples (Acts 17:24) and its statues of silver and gold (Acts 17:29). Paul knew what it meant to put his trust in the Lord. He wrote in his letter to the Romans, "If God is for us, who can be against us?" (Rom. 8:31).

* * *

EVEN IN PRISON, Paul praised the Lord (Acts 16:25).

* * *

ON ONE OCCASION (Acts 22:1–24) in Jerusalem, a riotous crowd was out to kill him. Soldiers intervened to save his life. Paul took the opportunity to *preach another sermon* about Jesus Christ.

* * *

NOTHING STOPPED PAUL from his mission—not ridicule, not slander, not prison, not beatings, not shipwreck, not being stoned, not even the "thorn in his flesh" (2 Cor. 12:7). In reviewing all these problems, he said God's power was made perfect in contrast to his own weakness.

Also, in reviewing his futile attempts to keep the Law, he saw they amounted to "nothing at all" (garbage) when compared to his task of preaching Jesus Christ to the world (Phil. 3:4–11).

Paul had the right attitude:

- He believed God's grace was sufficient for him (2 Cor. 12:9).

- He considered it an honor to suffer for the name of Jesus (2 Cor. 12:10).

- He refused to despair (2 Cor. 4:8).

- He had a glorious hope (Rom. 8:18).

God help us have the same attitude.

* * *

Day 3

PAUL REMAINED FAITHFUL to the end. I look forward to seeing him in heaven (2 Tim. 4:7–8).

* * *

WHEN THINKING about the lost condition of the enemies of Christ, Paul was moved to tears. His pity and sorrow can be an example for us. Perhaps such deep concern for the lost would guide us to be more aggressive in our mission to the world (Phil. 3:18).

* * *

IN ORDER to win more people to Christ, Paul was willing to do anything (1 Cor. 9:19–23).

* * *

IMMEDIATELY upon his conversion, the will of Saul (Paul) was changed (converted). He had vigorously opposed the church. Now he asks, "What wilt thou have me to do?" (Acts 9:6 KJV).

* * *

FREQUENTLY GOD SENDS another person to help us, just as Ananias was sent to heal Paul (Acts 9:17). Are you willing and open for God to use you as the "human instrument" to help and bless someone?

* * *

PAUL WAS MOVED to witness. Why? Because the Spirit of God was in him.

*   *   *

SOME PEOPLE find it most difficult to witness to relatives. Paul goes to his hometown (Acts 9:30). By the same Spirit, you and I can witness to relatives.

*   *   *

Day 4

THE DISTANCE from Jerusalem to Damascus is approximately 140 miles, a week's journey by foot. It was a life-changing trip for Paul.

The message of Paul was always clear and sharp. No one had to wonder what he meant. Had he "softened" his message, people would have been confused about grace. Paul wanted them to understand clearly—there is only one way to be saved, and that is by grace through faith in Jesus Christ.

He did not compromise the message to fit the world. Compromise makes you ineffective for the Lord. Ineffective people are not persecuted. Paul experienced many vicious attacks. He considered such attacks a blessing because they taught him that he must rely totally on God (2 Cor. 1:9).

Like Paul, you have to make a choice. Either you "tickle" the ears with half-truths, or you "tingle" the ears with the truth.

*   *   *

GOD DOES NOT HOLD past sins against us—once they are forgiven in Christ they are gone forever. It is a new day. You are a new person. Serve the Lord in gladness. (See Key Chapter booklet *Romans 6: New Life*.)

* * *

IN ACTS 9:13 AND 41 the word sometimes translated "believers" means "saints." Later Paul often uses this same word to describe those who follow Christ. The word literally means "holy ones." Those who have been chosen by God are sanctified—made holy—by God. They have joy! They have purpose! They have hope! Eternity is theirs!

* * *

THE FOLLOWERS OF JESUS were first called "Christians" at Antioch (Acts 11:26). To this day Christians give glory to God by proudly bearing his name and giving public testimony to their being followers of Christ.

* * *

Day 5

SOME OF MY FAVORITE PASSAGES from Paul's letters include the following:

* * *

ROM. 6:23: **For the wages of sin is death, but the gift of God is eternal life in Christ Jesus our Lord.**

1 Cor. 15:20–23, 42–44, 51–52: **But Christ has indeed been raised from the dead, the firstfruits of those who have fallen asleep. For since death came through a man, the resurrection of the dead comes also through a man. For as in Adam all die, so in Christ all will be made alive. But each in his own turn: Christ, the firstfruits; then, when he comes, those who belong to him.**

So will it be with the resurrection of the dead. The body that is sown is perishable, it is raised imperishable; it is sown in dishonor, it is raised in glory; it is sown in weakness, it is raised in power; it is sown a natural body, it is raised a spiritual body.

Listen, I tell you a mystery: We will not all sleep, but we will all be changed—in a flash, in the twinkling of an eye, at the last trumpet. For the trumpet will sound, the dead will be raised imperishable, and we will be changed.

*   *   *

Gal. 2:19–20: **For through the law I died to the law so that I might live for God. I have been crucified with Christ and I no longer live, but Christ lives in me. The life I live in the body, I live by faith in the Son of God, who loved me and gave himself for me.**

*   *   *

Eph. 2:8–10: **For it is by grace you have been saved, through faith—and this not from yourselves, it is the gift of God—not by works, so that no one can boast. For we are God's workmanship, created in**

Christ Jesus to do good works, which God prepared in advance for us to do.

*   *   *

PHIL. 4:4–7: Rejoice in the Lord always. I will say it again: Rejoice! Let your gentleness be evident to all. The Lord is near. Do not be anxious about anything, but in everything, by prayer and petition, with thanksgiving, present your requests to God. And the peace of God, which transcends all understanding, will guard your hearts and your minds in Christ Jesus.

*   *   *

1 THESS. 4:13–18: Brothers, we do not want you to be ignorant about those who fall asleep, or to grieve like the rest of men, who have no hope. We believe that Jesus died and rose again and so we believe that God will bring with Jesus those who have fallen asleep in him. According to the Lord's own word, we tell you that we who are still alive, who are left till the coming of the Lord, will certainly not precede those who have fallen asleep. For the Lord himself will come down from heaven, with a loud command, with the voice of the archangel and with the trumpet call of God, and the dead in Christ will rise first. After that, we who are still alive and are left will be caught up together with them in the clouds to meet the Lord in the air. And so we will be with the Lord forever. Therefore encourage each other with these words.

1 Tim. 1:15–16: **Here is a trustworthy saying that deserves full acceptance: Christ Jesus came into the world to save sinners—of whom I am the worst. But for that very reason I was shown mercy so that in me, the worst of sinners, Christ Jesus might display his unlimited patience as an example for those who would believe on him and receive eternal life.**

*   *   *

2 Tim. 1:7–9: **For God did not give us a spirit of timidity, but a spirit of power, of love and of self-discipline. So do not be ashamed to testify about our Lord, or ashamed of me his prisoner. But join with me in suffering for the gospel, by the power of God, who has saved us and called us to a holy life—not because of anything we have done but because of his own purpose and grace.**

*   *   *

Titus 2:11–14: **For the grace of God that brings salvation has appeared to all men. It teaches us to say "No" to ungodliness and worldly passions, and to live self-controlled, upright and godly lives in this present age, while we wait for the blessed hope—the glorious appearing of our great God and Savior, Jesus Christ, who gave himself for us to redeem us from all wickedness and to purify for himself a people that are his very own, eager to do what is good.**

*   *   *

PHILEMON 6: **I pray that you may be active in sharing your faith, so that you will have a full understanding of every good thing we have in Christ.**